THE INTERACTIONS OF JESUS ACCORDING TO THE
GOSPEL OF MATTHEW

THE GREATEST LEADER OF ALL TIME

JEAN KABASOMI

Copyright © 2020 by Jean Kabasomi.

Jean Kabasomi has asserted her right under the Copyright, Designs and Patents Act, 1988, to be identified as author of this work.

Unless otherwise indicated, all Scripture quotations are taken from The Holy Bible, New Living Translation (NLT), copyright © 1996, 2004, 2007, 2013, 2015 by Tyndale House Foundation. Used by permission of Tyndale House Publishers, Inc., Carol Stream, Illinois 60188. All rights reserved. Used by permission.

Other Scripture quotations are taken from:
The King James Version of the Bible (KJV), public domain.
The Holy Bible, New International Version® (NIV). Copyright © 1973, 1978, 1984, 2011 by Biblica Inc. Used by permission of Zondervan Publishing House. All rights reserved.
The Message® (MSG). Copyright © 1993, 1994, 1995, 1996, 2000, 2001, 2002. Used by permission of NavPress Publishing Group.
The New King James Version® (NKJV). Copyright © 1982 by Thomas Nelson, Inc. Used by permission. All rights reserved.
The New American Standard Bible® (NASB). Copyright © 1960, 1962, 1963, 1968, 1971, 1972, 1973, 1975, 1977, 1995 by The Lockman Foundation. Used by permission. www.Lockman.org.

Cover Design by 100Covers.com
Interior Design by FormattedBooks.com

CONTENTS

Acknowledgements..V
Preface...VII

Introduction..1
Chapter 1: A disciple is not above his master 7
Chapter 2: Jesus' interactions with God the Father 9
Chapter 3: Jesus' interactions with his disciples 20
Chapter 4: Jesus' interactions with Judas 46
Chapter 5: Jesus' interations with minor characters 54
Chapter 6: Jesus' interactions with the Pharisees.....................72
Chapter 7: What did Jesus do when he was alone?....................96
Conclusion 109

Epilogue 111

ACKNOWLEDGEMENTS

I would obviously and most importantly like to thank God for this book. I have never written one and I believe it was only by his grace that I have been able to write it in such a short time (I wrote this book in its entirety during the 2020 national lockdown period in the UK).

I would also like to thank Lady Pastor Margaret Pierre, Pastor Gaius Nyarko and Erica Deti for reading the initial drafts and providing invaluable feedback. God bless you for your patience and time.

Finally, I would like to thank my editor, Pamela Skipwith, for her guidance and direction on this project.

PREFACE

I have often been told that I should write a book, but never knew what to write about, so I am just as surprised as anyone that I managed to write a book during the 2020 COVID-19 pandemic 'lockdown' period in the UK.

Although writing a book on leadership, I make no claims to being a successful leader with a large organisation; neither do I have a list of credentials that makes me qualified to write this book. However, in the interest of full disclosure, I do have a bachelor's degree in theology from Durham University and a master's degree in Biblical Studies from the University of Edinburgh. What I do also have is my belief in the power of an effective quiet time and the leading of the Holy Spirit to turn my quiet times into a book.[1]

This book is based on my personal revelations from my daily quiet times, considering the leadership qualities of Jesus Christ from the

---

1   For further insight on the topic of quiet times, see Dag Heward-Mills, *How You Can Have an Effective Quiet Time with God Every Day* (London: Parchment House, 2017).

Gospel of Matthew. I pray that whatever insight is written in these pages will encourage you and have a positive impact in your walk with Christ.

God bless you,
Jean

INTRODUCTION

Why write a book about Jesus Christ and leadership? The answer is extremely simple – no person whether male or female has had as great or greater impact on human civilisation than Jesus Christ. Without going into too much detail, Jesus Christ has amassed one of the largest numbers of followers in history. He has impacted different people from all walks of life, across all continents, time periods and expertise. Whether it be literature, media, film, science, arts, politics, religion, history, business, education, charity or music – the impact of Jesus Christ and his ministry can be and has been felt.[2] I am always

---

2   **Christ figures are present in the following (not an exhaustive list):** **Literature** – Harry Potter in the Harry Potter Series – Jonathan Petre, 'J.K. Rowling, "Christianity inspired Harry Potter"', *The Telegraph*, 20 October 2017, www.telegraph.co.uk/culture/books/fictionreviews/3668658/J-K-Rowling-Christianity-inspired-Harry-Potter.html. Aslan – in C.S. Lewis', *The Lion, Witch and the Wardrobe*, J.R. Tolkien, *The Lord of the Rings*. **Film** – 'Neo in The Wachowskis', *Matrix* series; Batman in Christopher Nolan's *The Dark Knight Rises*; Iron Man in The Russo Brothers', *Avengers: Endgame*. **People or organisations influenced by Jesus Christ**: **Science** – George Washington Carver (1860s–1943), agricultural chemist and botanist, believed his relationship with Jesus influenced his work, and he often paraphrased John

surprised when I watch a film where the main character sacrifices himself for the salvation of the world.

> 8:32 to 'And you shall know science and science shall make you free.' – The Free Library. S.v. 'Man of science—and of God: George Washington Carver believed that Providence guided his scientific investigations and that those investigations led to a better understanding of God and His handiwork', www.thefreelibrary.com/Man+of+science—and+of+God%3a+George+Washington+Carver+believed+that...-a0112794990. **Arts** – Michelangelo, Raphael and Rembrandt all painted masterpieces depicting a scene from the life of Jesus Christ. **Music** – Bach, Handel and Mozart all wrote infamous classical pieces influenced by Jesus. Gospel and Contemporary Christian Music are two genres dedicated and solely created to describe the impact of Jesus in the life of the artists. Additionally, a number of modern mainstream artists including U2, Lenny Kravitz and Kanye West have all written music describing the influence of Jesus Christ in their lives. **Politics** – William Wilberforce, the anti-slavery politician, said 'I would suggest that faith is everyone's business. The advance or decline of faith is so intimately connected to the welfare of a society that it should be of particular interest to a politician.' 'Surely the principles of Christianity lead to action as well as meditation.' **Business** – Forever 21 shopping bags make reference to John 3:16. **Education** – Many of the best universities in the world were founded on the principle of searching for truth in Jesus Christ. Example: Extract from Harvard University's Rules and Precepts (1646) – '*2. Let every Student be plainly instructed, and earnestly pressed to consider well, the maine end of his life and studies is, to know God and Jesus Christ which is eternal life (John 17:3) and therefore to lay Christ in the bottome, as the only foundation of all sound knowledge and Learning. And seeing the Lord only giveth wisedome, Let every one seriously set himself by prayer in secret to seeke it of him (Prov. 2:3).*' – Harvard GSAS Christian Community, www.hcs.harvard.edu/~gsascf/shield-and-veritas-history/. **Charities**: World Vision and Open Doors are international Christian charities. Samaritans, although not a Christian charity, has a name taken from the parable of the Good Samaritan in Luke 10:25–37. [All links accessed 28 July 2020.]

One does not have to be a Christian to learn from, identify or acknowledge the impact Jesus Christ has left on humanity. His words and actions were ahead of his time in so many aspects. For example, today it doesn't seem like much of a big deal for Jesus' parables to have female characters, or that he addressed women directly in his ministry.[3] But when one compares him with his contemporaries, it is clear he was a true pioneer.

Leaving aside his personal impact, his disciples themselves left a lasting legacy on the communities and nations they visited; an impact so great that many today in our social media-driven world could only dream of and envy it. Perhaps the most prominent disciple is the Apostle Peter, whose church still stands as one of the largest organisations in the world today in terms of both members and wealth.[4]

Even the CEOs of the biggest companies in the world today should be impressed or at least intrigued by a legacy that stretches over 2,000 years, has impacted billions of people and been influential in the formation of multiple organisations and charities across different sectors in every corner of the world.

---

3   This was first brought to my attention in a module I took at Durham University by Dr William Telford, entitled *Jesus in Fiction and Film*. Examples include the parable of the Ten Virgins – Matthew 25:1–13; the Syrophoenician Woman – Mark 7:24–30; the parable of the Lost Coin – Luke 15:8–10; the parable of the Persistent Widow – Luke 18:1–8; the Woman of Samaria – John 4:1–42.

4   According to the Vatican's statistics, as of 31 December 2017 there were 1.3 billion Catholics in the world, www.fides.org/en/news/66809-VATICAN_Catholic_Church_Statistics_2019. An exact figure for the total wealth of the Catholic Church is difficult to find. But the Church owns vast amounts of priceless art, real estate and land estimated to be worth billions in the Vatican City State alone.

For those of us in the Christian faith, understanding the leadership qualities of Jesus Christ can help us build a stronger, better and more productive Church. In doing this, we can hope to raise disciples with the same characteristics, determination and zeal as the original apostles.

Before going any further, it is worth addressing the elephant in the room. For many atheists and agonists assert that religion, and more specifically Christianity and therefore by extension Jesus Christ, has been responsible for more war and persecution in human history than any other thing. I disagree with this; the truth is people can and will manipulate anything to suit their own agendas and to gain power. If one reads the words of Jesus rationally, intelligently and within context, it is almost unthinkable that one could be led to attack, murder or kill another human being.[5]

To use a modern example, during the pandemic governments around the world issued nationwide lockdowns. The lockdowns were intended to protect people and prevent the spread of COVID-19. However, there have been reports that illicit criminal behaviour has increased on the Dark Web, as has domestic violence.[6] What was meant to be a good thing has been used to facilitate evil and crime. I would argue the same thing has been done with Christianity, to varying degrees, throughout history. We would not and do not dismiss the use of the lockdown because some have exploited it for their own wicked agendas; using the same logic, we should not dismiss the teachings and life of Jesus because some have misused it for gain.

---

5   This for me includes the years of persecution and anti-Semitism inflicted on Jews in the name of avenging the crucifixion of Jesus.
6   Mike Thompson, 'Online child abuse rising during lockdown warn police', *BBC News*, 29 May 2020, www.bbc.co.uk/news/world-52773344.

While writing this book, my greatest discoveries have been where I have seen Jesus do or say things which are contrary to what I know to be '*good leadership*'. There have been moments which read contrary to traditional wisdom and ways of doing things; perhaps it is these differences which have made Jesus' way of doings different from most if not all of us. Perhaps it is these differences which have contributed to his sustainability and spurred his disciples on to deliver his teachings and story with such vigour and passion to all they came in contact with? Perhaps it is these differences which make him the greatest leader of all time!

CHAPTER 1

A DISCIPLE IS NOT ABOVE HIS MASTER

> Matthew 10:24 – The disciple is not above his master, nor the servant above his lord. (KJV)

As Christians, we often expect that life will be a bed of roses and the people we meet will always bless and favour us. We embrace the good things found in the Bible and anticipate prosperity. Our go-to verses are *'the LORD will make you the head and not the tail'* (Deuteronomy 28:13, NKJV), *I am blessed on every side* (Job 1:10), *My enemies are defeated* (Psalm 54:5), but in doing this we forget the person whom we are following did not always live these confessions. Many of us backslide and reject God because the people we encounter and our life experiences do not tally with our expectations and confessions.

In his thirty-three years on this earth, Jesus interacted with a variety of different personalities and characters who impacted his mission, journey and life. He encountered good and wicked people. He had friends and traitors, supporters and haters. In our walk with Christ, as his followers, we can and should only expect to encounter the same sort of people because, as Jesus taught us, the disciple is not above his master.

> **Matthew 10:24 – The disciple is not above his master, nor the servant above his lord. (KJV)**

This book seeks to forensically examine Jesus' interactions with people from all walks of life – the good, bad and the ugly. The great and small, the rich and poor. By investigating Jesus' interactions and relationships, we can build a picture of his leadership style and qualities. It is my prayer that you will be able to apply the leadership style of Jesus to your life and ministry so that you can overcome the distractions and disappointments so many of us encounter as we embark on what we believe God has called us to fulfil in our lifetime.

CHAPTER 2

JESUS' INTERACTIONS WITH GOD THE FATHER

Before we look at Jesus' interactions with people, it is only fitting that we first examine his relationship with God the Father. The Gospel of Matthew makes reference to only two specific moments where Jesus interacts with his Father. This in itself is striking; one might expect that God the Father and Jesus would regularly commune throughout the Gospel. But when we examine the words of Jesus this should actually come as no surprise to us. In this chapter, we will look at both the implicit and explicit interactions between God the Father and Jesus Christ.

To be clear, the implicit interactions are those where we have to assume there must have been an interaction between two beings or entities. The explicit interactions are those where Jesus directly addresses God the Father.

The implicit interactions with God the Father

1) The words of Jesus

When we examine the words of Jesus, we find he spoke widely about the opinion of God the Father on a number of different topics. Not only did he offer opinions of the Father, he spoke on behalf of the Father.

> **Matthew 6:1 – Watch out! Don't do your good deeds publicly, to be admired by others, for you will lose the reward from your Father in heaven.**
>
> **Matthew 6:4 – Give your gifts in private, and your Father, who sees everything, will reward you.**
>
> **Matthew 6:6 – But when you pray, go away by yourself, shut the door behind you, and pray to your Father in private. Then your Father, who sees everything, will reward you.**
>
> **Matthew 6:8 – Don't be like them, for your Father knows exactly what you need even before you ask him!**
>
> **Matthew 6:14-15 – If you forgive those who sin against you, your heavenly Father will forgive you. But if you refuse to forgive others, your Father will not forgive your sins.**
>
> **Matthew 6:32 – These things dominate the thoughts of unbelievers, but your heavenly Father already knows all your needs.**
>
> **Matthew 15:13 – Jesus replied, 'Every plant not planted by my heavenly Father will be uprooted,'**
>
> **Matthew 18:35 – That's what my heavenly Father will do to you if you refuse to forgive your brothers and sisters from your heart.**

From this we can glean that an unseen or unreported relationship existed between the two. Our everyday human relationships tell us a person cannot presume to speak on someone's behalf if they do not know them.

An ambassador speaks on behalf of the country, given their relationship with the head of state. A personal assistant knows how their boss wants things done because of their regular and constant interaction and strong relationship.

We should not be surprised that the relationship between the Father and Son was strong but unseen, because that is precisely what Jesus told us to do. Jesus taught us to pray in our closet in secret and it is then that the Father will reward us.

> Matthew 6:5-6 – When you pray, don't be like the hypocrites who love to pray publicly on street corners and in the synagogues where everyone can see them. I tell you the truth, that is all the reward they will ever get. But when you pray, go away by yourself, shut the door behind you, and pray to your Father in private. Then your Father, who sees everything, will reward you.

As we will see in the following chapters, this is not the only example of Jesus practising what he preached.

2) *The baptism of Jesus and transfiguration*

Matthew 3:16–17–After his baptism, as Jesus came up out of the water, the heavens were opened and he saw the Spirit of God descending like a dove and settling on him. And a voice from heaven said, 'This is my dearly loved Son, who brings me great joy.'

> Matthew 17:1–5 – Six days later Jesus took Peter and the two brothers, James and John, and led them up a high mountain to be alone. As the men watched, Jesus' appearance was transformed so that his face shone like the sun, and his clothes became as white as light. Suddenly, Moses and Elijah appeared and began talking with Jesus. Peter exclaimed, 'Lord, it's wonderful for us to be here! If you want, I'll make three shelters as memorials—one for you, one for Moses, and one for Elijah.' But even as he spoke, a bright cloud overshadowed them, and a voice from the cloud said, 'This is my dearly loved Son, who brings me great joy. Listen to him.'

Again, in both of these examples from the Scriptures, the Father and the Son do not interact directly. What we see is the Father stamping his approval on Jesus in public.

> Matthew 3:17 – And a voice from heaven said, 'This is my dearly loved Son, who brings me great joy.'

> Matthew 17:5 – But even as he spoke, a bright cloud overshadowed them, and a voice from the cloud said, 'This is my dearly loved Son, who brings me great joy. Listen to him.'

Perhaps these supernatural encounters were a fulfilment of the Father rewarding the Son openly because of his secret relationship.

> Matthew 6:6 – But when you pray, go away by yourself, shut the door behind you, and pray to your Father in private. Then your Father, who sees everything, will reward you.

We often attribute these experiences to Jesus' godly nature, but if we view them in light of his humanity and understand them as his reward for obedience to the principle of secret prayer, we may gain insight into a channel the Father uses to promote us.

The method that God the Father uses to reward and fulfil our vision and purpose is the same for us as it was for Jesus. If we are able and willing to develop our relationship with God the Father in secret, we will be rewarded openly.

> Isaiah 1:19 – If ye be willing and obedient, ye shall eat the good of the land. (KJV)

The explicit interactions with God the Father

1) The Garden of Gethsemane

It is worth noting the explicit references to Jesus' interactions with God the Father occurred at his weakest moments. At the first in the Garden of Gethsemane, Jesus withdrew from his disciples and went to pray.

> Matthew 26:39 – He went on a little farther and bowed with his face to the ground, praying, 'My Father! If it is possible, let this cup of suffering be taken away from me. Yet I want your will to be done, not mine.'

> Matthew 26:42 – Then Jesus left them a second time and prayed, 'My Father! If this cup cannot be taken away unless I drink it, your will be done.'

As he taught his disciples earlier in the Gospel, he prayed for the will of God to be done.

> Matthew 6:9–10 – Pray like this: Our Father in heaven, may your name be kept holy. May your Kingdom come soon. May your will be done on earth, as it is in heaven.

In the midst of difficulty when the promise looks as if it will not be fulfilled, we must remember to pray for the will of God to be done. Notice Jesus prayed this prayer at least three times in the garden.

> **Matthew 26:39** – He went on a little farther and bowed with his face to the ground, praying, 'My Father! If it is possible, let this cup of suffering be taken away from me. Yet I want your will to be done, not mine.'

> **Matthew 26:42** – Then Jesus left them a second time and prayed, 'My Father! If this cup cannot be taken away unless I drink it, your will be done.'

> **Matthew 26:44** – So he went to pray a third time, saying the same things again.

After praying for the will of God, we must learn to accept our circumstances are the answer to our prayer, whether they are good or bad. This is obviously more difficult when the outcome is not what we are expecting. But we must remember that it was Christ's obedience to death on the cross which led to his exaltation.

> **Philippians 2:7–11** – Instead, he gave up his divine privileges; he took the humble position of a slave and was born as a human being. When he appeared in human form, he humbled himself in obedience to God and died a criminal's death on a cross. Therefore, God elevated him to the place of highest honor and gave him the name above all other names, that at the name of Jesus every knee should bow, in heaven and on earth and under the earth, and every tongue declare that Jesus Christ is Lord, to the glory of God the Father.

Christ must have believed the circumstances he found himself in were an answer to his prayers and therefore God's will or else he would have reacted. He would have acted in such a way as to alter what was going on around him. We have seen him intervene in circumstances to change the outcome elsewhere – remember the fig tree!

> **Matthew 21:18–19 – In the morning, as Jesus was returning to Jerusalem, he was hungry, and he noticed a fig tree beside the road. He went over to see if there were any figs, but there were only leaves. Then he said to it, 'May you never bear fruit again!' And immediately the fig tree withered up.**

Not only did he succumb to the situation he found himself in, but he also prevented those around him from intervening and altering it.

> **Matthew 26:50–54 – Jesus said, 'My friend, go ahead and do what you have come for.' Then the others grabbed Jesus and arrested him. But one of the men with Jesus pulled out his sword and struck the high priest's slave, slashing off his ear. 'Put away your sword,' Jesus told him. 'Those who use the sword will die by the sword. Don't you realize that I could ask my Father for thousands of angels to protect us, and he would send them instantly? But if I did, how would the Scriptures be fulfilled that describe what must happen now?'**

We must constantly ask ourselves whether our circumstances are in fact the will of God, especially when they are different from what we are expecting to hear from God. We must examine whether we should be resisting or accepting our situation. Perhaps God is trying to teach me something here? We must ask ourselves whether this is the route to our glory or fruitfulness.

> **John 12:24 – Verily, verily, I say unto you, Except a corn of wheat fall into the ground and die, it abideth alone: but if it die, it bringeth forth much fruit. (KJV)**

Another lesson to learn from Jesus here is that his sharing of his difficulty with the disciples (friends) did not stop or prevent him from going to God the Father.

> **Matthew 26:37-39 – He took Peter and Zebedee's two sons, James and John, and he became anguished and distressed. He told them, 'My soul is crushed with grief to the point of death. Stay here and keep watch with me.' He went on a little farther and bowed with his face to the ground, praying, 'My Father! If it is possible, let this cup of suffering be taken away from me. Yet I want your will to be done, not mine.'**

As leaders, we must not forget to share our struggles and difficulties with the Father in prayer, even if we have already shared them with friends.

2) *The cross*

> **Matthew 27:46 – At about three o'clock, Jesus called out with a loud voice, '*Eli, Eli, lema sabachthani?*' which means 'My God, my God, why have you abandoned me?'**

The second explicit interaction between the Father and the Son took place at the cross. It is in this interaction that we truly see the humanity of Christ. Just as so many of us have experienced, Christ at his weakest and lowest point felt abandoned by God the Father. If the Son of God felt rejected and neglected by God the Father, then we can certainly expect to feel the same thing!

> **Matthew 10:24 – A disciple is not above his teacher, nor a servant above his master. (NKJV)**

We are allowed to and should express our feelings before God. The Psalms of David are littered with expressions of lament, worry and disappointment.

> **Psalm 22:1 – My God, my God, why have you abandoned me? Why are you so far away when I groan for help?**
>
> **Psalm 13:2 – How long must I struggle with anguish in my soul, with sorrow in my heart every day? How long will my enemy have the upper hand?**
>
> **Psalm 10:1 – O Lord, why do you stand so far away? Why do you hide when I am in trouble?**

Job and the prophets of the Old Testament constantly describe their suffering and pain, while the book of Lamentations is devoted entirely to the misery felt after the destruction of Jerusalem.

> **Job 3:11 – Why wasn't I born dead? Why didn't I die as I came from the womb?**
>
> **Jeremiah 15:18 – Why then does my suffering continue? Why is my wound so incurable? Your help seems as uncertain as a seasonal brook, like a spring that has gone dry.**

Such expressions describing the anguish we feel are not questions of faith but, rather, questions of humanity.

Sometimes we share these feelings of humanity with other people instead of with God, which can lead to more problems than it solves. Sharing these feelings with the wrong person can lead to our being misunderstood, which in turn can cause us to question our faith and commitment to God. This is simply because we get the wrong reaction from the person with whom we have shared our deepest and innermost thoughts.

People can be (often unintentionally) dismissive of our pain and feelings, which can in turn cause us to give up on God's promises and, in extreme cases, abandon our faith altogether. I have frequently heard of Christians who have given up their faith because their response to a challenge was not what they had been told it ought to be. They suddenly feel Christianity is not for them because they have not responded in the way in which they should.

I am not saying that we should not seek counsel or help when needed; Jesus himself confided in the disciples before he went to the cross.

> **Matthew 26:1-2 – When Jesus had finished saying all these things, he said to his disciples, 'As you know, Passover begins in two days, and the Son of Man will be handed over to be crucified.'**

> **Matthew 26:37-39 – He took Peter and Zebedee's two sons, James and John, and he became anguished and distressed. He told them, 'My soul is crushed with grief to the point of death. Stay here and keep watch with me.' He went on a little farther and bowed with his face to the ground, praying, 'My Father! If it is possible, let this cup of suffering be taken away from me. Yet I want your will to be done, not mine.'**

But there is a season and time when we ought to cast our cares and burdens on him.

> **Psalm 55:22 – Give your burdens to the LORD, and he will take care of you. He will not permit the godly to slip and fall.**

In doing this, rather than turning to people alone, our burdens are made light.

> **Matthew 11:28–30 – Then Jesus said, 'Come to me, all of you who are weary and carry heavy burdens, and I will give you rest. Take my yoke upon you. Let me teach you, because I am humble and gentle at heart, and you will find rest for your souls. For my yoke is easy to bear, and the burden I give you is light.'**

It is worth noting that in both instances, in Gethsemane and at the cross, Jesus did not get a direct response from God the Father. This is generally the same for us. Often, we pray, call on God and get no response. The silence can be deafening. However, in these moments we ought to remember, like Jesus, the very circumstances we find ourselves in could quite possibly be the very answer we are looking for.

CHAPTER 3

JESUS' INTERACTIONS WITH HIS DISCIPLES

While Jesus associated with a number of different characters throughout the Gospel of Matthew, he spent most of his time with his disciples. In this chapter we will look at the lessons on leadership that can be learnt from the many interactions Jesus had with his disciples.

> Matthew 4:18–20 – One day as Jesus was walking along the shore of the Sea of Galilee, he saw two brothers—Simon, also called Peter, and Andrew—throwing a net into the water, for they fished for a living. Jesus called out to them, 'Come, follow me, and I will show you how to fish for people!' And they left their nets at once and followed him.
>
> Matthew 4:21–22 – A little farther up the shore he saw two other brothers, James and John, sitting in a boat with their father, Zebedee, repairing their nets. And he called them to come, too. They immediately followed him, leaving the boat and their father behind.

1) Don't be surprised if you find yourself working with people with similar backgrounds

We should not be surprised if we constantly find ourselves working with the same sort of people. Jesus spoke to two sets of brothers and both followed. There is no need to be ashamed if you have many like-minded people following you. This could be the group of people you have been specifically called to minister to or the type of people who are best suited to be your helpers.

> **Matthew 4:18 – One day as Jesus was walking along the shore of the Sea of Galilee, he *saw two brothers—Simon, also called Peter, and Andrew.*[7]**

> **Matthew 4:21 – A little farther up the shore he saw *two other brothers, James and John.***

When God created Eve, he described her as a helper suitable for Adam.

> **Genesis 2:18 – Then the LORD God said, 'It is not good for the man to be alone. I will make a helper who is just right [suitable] for him.'**

Perhaps these people are the helpers God has ordained as being just right for you.

2) A person's calling or dream may be linked to a group

Often, we make the point that the call is an individual affair but, in these two instances in Matthew chapter 4, we see that Jesus called a pair of brothers. Although speculative, it is worth asking ourselves whether

---

7   All use of italics through quoted text is to show the author's emphasis.

James and John would be the same disciples we know, had they not both responded at the same time to the call of God.

Sometimes, our calling may be tied to someone other than a mentor or father. It may in fact be related to a colleague, co-equal, friend or sibling. That is not to say it is dependent on that individual, since the disciples all walked in their own callings subsequent to the initial call from the Lord.

But it cannot be denied there is something significant about both the timing and relationship between the brothers who were called at the same time. This is further highlighted by the fact Jesus also called individuals to join the twelve. Would the disciples be the disciples we know today, if there had not been a group of twelve?

3) *You can find people who are attracted to your vision who will immediately stop what they are doing and follow you*

> **Matthew 4:20 – And they left their nets at once and followed him.**
>
> **Matthew 4:22 – They immediately followed him, leaving the boat and their father behind.**

Jesus did not struggle to recruit the disciples. He literally spoke a few words to them and they dropped what they were doing and followed him. There will be some people who find the proposition of following you and working with you attractive and will stop what they are doing to work with you. Value those who fall into this category, as these will be the people who will support you and push your vision forward in your absence.

These disciples supported and helped Jesus throughout his ministry and continued to spread his message when he left.

4) The call of God usually applies to an individual

> **Matthew 9:9 – As Jesus was walking along, he saw a man named Matthew sitting at his tax collector's booth. *'Follow me and be my disciple,'* Jesus said to him. So, Matthew got up and followed him.**

While Peter and Andrew and James and John were called as two pairs of brothers, Matthew was called as an individual.[8]

5) Joining a team later does not make you any less of a player

> **Matthew 9:9–10 – As Jesus was walking along, he saw a man named Matthew sitting at his tax collector's booth. 'Follow me and be my disciple,' Jesus said to him. So, Matthew got up and followed him. Later, Matthew invited Jesus and his disciples to his home as dinner guests, along with many tax collectors and other disreputable sinners.**

Matthew was called to join after a group of disciples had already been formed. Despite coming to them later, he was not seen as any lesser than the others. This is a principle Jesus taught his disciples in the parable of the vineyard workers.

> **Matthew 20:1–16 – For the kingdom of heaven is like a landowner who went out early in the morning to hire laborers for his vineyard. Now when he had agreed with the laborers for a denarius a day, he sent them into his vineyard. And he went out about the third hour and saw others standing idle in the marketplace, and said to them, 'You also go into the vineyard, and whatever is right I will give you.' So they went. Again he went out about the sixth and the ninth hour, and did**

---

[8] We can only assume the remaining seven disciples were also called individually, given that this is a common theme throughout the Bible e.g.: Abraham – Genesis 12:1 and Paul – Acts 9:4–6; 15–16.

likewise. And about the eleventh hour he went out and found others standing idle, and said to them, 'Why have you been standing here idle all day?' They said to him, 'Because no one hired us.' He said to them, 'You also go into the vineyard, and whatever is right you will receive.'

So when evening had come, the owner of the vineyard said to his steward, 'Call the laborers and give them their wages, beginning with the last to the first.' And when those came who were hired about the eleventh hour, they each received a denarius. But when the first came, they supposed that they would receive more; and they likewise received each a denarius.

And when they had received it, they complained against the landowner, saying, 'These last men have worked only one hour, and you made them equal to us who have borne the burden and the heat of the day.' But he answered one of them and said, 'Friend, I am doing you no wrong. Did you not agree with me for a denarius? Take what is yours and go your way. I wish to give to this last man the same as to you. Is it not lawful for me to do what I wish with my own things? Or is your eye evil because I am good?'

So the last will be first, and the first last. For many are called, but few chosen. (NKJV)

Many times, Matthew 20:16 is quoted to emphasise the point that those who arrive first will be overtaken by those who came last, alongside a partial quotation of Ecclesiastes 9:11.

> Ecclesiastes 9:11 – *I returned, and saw under the sun, that the race is not to the swift, nor the battle to the strong, neither yet bread to the wise, nor yet riches to men of understanding, nor yet favour to men of skill;* but time and chance happeneth to them all. (KJV)

However, if Matthew 20:16 is read in light of the rest of the parable, the message Jesus was trying to convey was that it doesn't really matter *when* you turn up to do the job. The reward agreed is the same for everyone, namely, the person who committed to do God's work earlier is exactly the same as the one who joined much later – their work is of equal value. The first guy is the same as the last and the last guy is the same as the first. Good leaders are able to foster and develop this culture of unconditionality within their teams.

6) *Position and rank are determined by God*

There were other disciples who were following Jesus before Matthew joined. We know this because some of the disciples had not previously been able to follow Jesus completely.

> **Matthew 8:18–19 – When Jesus saw the crowd around him, he instructed his *disciples* to cross to the other side of the lake. Then one of the teachers of religious law said to him, 'Teacher, I will follow you wherever you go.'**
>
> **Matthew 8:21 – Another of his *disciples* said, 'Lord, first let me return home and bury my father.'**

Despite this, Matthew was chosen as one of the twelve.

> **Matthew 10:2–4 – Jesus called his twelve disciples together and gave them authority to cast out evil spirits and to heal every kind of disease and illness. Here are the names of the twelve apostles: first, Simon (also called Peter), then Andrew (Peter's brother), James (son of Zebedee), John (James's brother), Philip, Bartholomew, Thomas, *Matthew (the tax collector)*, James (son of Alphaeus), Thaddaeus, Simon (the zealot), Judas Iscariot (who later betrayed him).**

There is no explanation as to why Matthew was given this position when he came *after* so many others who were already following Jesus. Perhaps the only explanation is that position is determined ultimately by God? It is not always clear why God chooses and selects people, but what is clear is that you do not have to join at the start of something for your worth to be valued.

7) Jesus was able to separate himself from his disciples to be alone with God the Father in times of prayer

> **Matthew 14:22–23 – Immediately after this, Jesus insisted that his disciples get back into the boat and cross to the other side of the lake, while he sent the people home. After sending them home, *he went up into the hills by himself to pray*. Night fell while he was there alone.**

Despite travelling and moving around with his disciples, Jesus was able to withdraw from them and pray. As Christian leaders, it is critical we find time to separate ourselves from the people we are leading in order to seek God.

8) A Christian leader must learn to trust in the sovereignty of God

> **Matthew 14:24–33 – Meanwhile, the disciples were in trouble far away from land, for a strong wind had risen, and they were fighting heavy waves. About three o'clock in the morning Jesus came toward them, walking on the water. When the disciples saw him walking on the water, they were terrified. In their fear, they cried out, 'It's a ghost!' But Jesus spoke to them at once. 'Don't be afraid,' he said. 'Take courage. I am here!'**
>
> **Then Peter called to him, 'Lord, if it's really you, tell me to come to you, walking on the water.' 'Yes, come,' Jesus said. So Peter went over the side of the boat and walked on the water toward Jesus. But when**

> he saw the strong wind and the waves, he was terrified and began to sink. 'Save me, Lord!' he shouted. Jesus immediately reached out and grabbed him. 'You have so little faith,' Jesus said. 'Why did you doubt me?' When they climbed back into the boat, the wind stopped. Then the disciples worshiped him. 'You really are the Son of God!' they exclaimed.

Sometimes we may ask God to help us with something and the answer is yes. But when a difficulty arises, we retreat from the promise out of fear. Peter asked Jesus if he could walk on the water. Jesus agreed to this but, as soon as Peter saw the strong wind and the waves, he began to sink.

Perhaps you have asked God if you can pursue a dream to start a business, become a worship leader or start a church but, at the first sign of difficulty, you have given up and retreated. Perhaps you have not had any customers for the first three months, you forgot the lyrics to a song you were leading or you are struggling to do effective evangelism because of a local natural disaster? These are not reasons to retreat. Peter's mistake was to look at the wind and waves rather than to fix his eyes on Jesus.

> **Hebrews 12:1-2 – Therefore, since we are surrounded by such a huge crowd of witnesses to the life of faith, let us strip off every weight that slows us down, especially the sin that so easily trips us up. And let us run with endurance the race God has set before us.** *We do this by keeping our eyes on Jesus*, **the champion who initiates and perfects our faith. Because of the joy awaiting him, he endured the cross, disregarding its shame. Now he is seated in the place of honor beside God's throne.**

Rather than look at the circumstances around us, we must focus on Jesus and remember that God is sovereign in all affairs.

> Daniel 4:17 – The angels announce this decree, the holy watchmen bring this sentence, So that everyone living will know that the High God rules human kingdoms. He arranges *kingdom affairs however he wishes, and makes leaders out of losers.* (MSG)

In spite of Peter's hiccup of faith, Jesus reached out to save him. To highlight God's sovereignty further, even when we are led by fear instead of faith, he will still reach out to save us and fulfil our requests.

> Matthew 14:31–32 – Jesus immediately reached out and grabbed him. 'You have so little faith,' Jesus said. 'Why did you doubt me?' When they climbed back into the boat, the wind stopped.

9) Good leaders find out what their followers think about them

> Matthew 16:13, 16:15–16 – When Jesus came to the region of Caesarea Philippi, he asked his disciples, 'Who do people say that the Son of Man is?' Then he asked them, 'But who do you say I am?' Simon Peter answered, 'You are the Messiah, the Son of the living God.'

Finding out what the people you work with think about you brings clarity to both you and them. It also allows for you to correct wrong mindsets or impressions about you.

10) Jesus had a core group of disciples he trusted and with whom he could be himself

> Matthew 17:1–9 – Six days later Jesus took Peter and the two brothers, James and John, and led them up a high mountain to be alone. As the men watched, Jesus' appearance was transformed so that his face shone like the sun, and his clothes became as white as light.
>
> Suddenly, Moses and Elijah appeared and began talking with Jesus. Peter exclaimed, 'Lord, it's wonderful for us to be here! If you want, I'll

> make three shelters as memorials—one for you, one for Moses, and one for Elijah.' But even as he spoke, a bright cloud overshadowed them, and a voice from the cloud said, 'This is my dearly loved Son, who brings me great joy. Listen to him.' The disciples were terrified and fell face down on the ground.
>
> Then Jesus came over and touched them. 'Get up,' he said. 'Don't be afraid.' And when they looked up, Moses and Elijah were gone, and they saw only Jesus. As they went back down the mountain, Jesus commanded them, 'Don't tell anyone what you have seen until the Son of Man has been raised from the dead.'

Jesus had three people with whom he could be himself. He separated Peter, James and John from the other disciples and revealed to them he was the Son of God. He must have trusted them greatly, as he believed they would be able to keep his secret until after his resurrection.

> Matthew 17:9 – As they went back down the mountain, Jesus commanded them, 'Don't tell anyone what you have seen until the Son of Man has been raised from the dead.'

Not only did he trust them with good secrets, but he revealed his emotions to them when he was at his weakest.

> Matthew 26:37–38 – He took Peter and Zebedee's two sons, James and John, and he became anguished and distressed. He told them, 'My soul is crushed with grief to the point of death. Stay here and keep watch with me.'

Jesus was able to reveal these secrets to the three disciples without fear of rejection. He was comfortable and knew them well enough to recognise they would not judge his weakness or overreact to his words. Every leader needs a core team where they can be themselves.

11) *Do not be disappointed if your followers put you in the wrong box*

> **Matthew 17:3-6 – Suddenly, Moses and Elijah appeared and began talking with Jesus. Peter exclaimed, 'Lord, it's wonderful for us to be here! If you want, *I'll make three shelters as memorials—one for you, one for Moses, and one for Elijah.*' But even as he spoke, a bright cloud overshadowed them, and a voice from the cloud said, 'This is my dearly loved Son, who brings me great joy. Listen to him.' The disciples were terrified and fell face down on the ground.**

At the transfiguration, Jesus' appearance changed. Moses and Elijah appeared and spoke with Jesus. When the disciples saw this, rather than think Jesus was different, they placed him in the same box as Moses and Elijah. Rather than thinking Jesus' uniqueness was the reason for Moses' and Elijah's appearance, they assumed the conversation meant the three were equal.

Peter genuinely thought he was doing the right thing when he suggested making a memorial to the three of them. He was happy to be there, excited that Jesus had selected them to see the transfiguration, but still missed the point of the supernatural encounter.

It took a voice from heaven to correct his error. God himself had to reveal to the disciples there was indeed a difference between Jesus and the Old Testament prophets.

Do not be disappointed or discouraged if your closest followers place you in a lower class than you deserve. Sometimes it takes a revelation from God himself for people to understand our true value. It is also worth noting that sometimes mistaken value statements are genuine mistakes. It is likely the people following you do believe in you, as was the case with Jesus and these three disciples, but they only have a partial understanding or revelation of your worth. Remember in the previous chapter, Peter had identified Jesus as the Messiah, yet he still made the mistake of equating Jesus with Moses and Elijah.

> **Matthew 16:16–17 – Simon Peter answered, 'You are the Messiah, the Son of the living God.' Jesus replied, 'You are blessed, Simon son of John, because my Father in heaven has revealed this to you. You did not learn this from any human being.'**

12) *Even after public correction, the disciples still found Jesus approachable*

> **Matthew 17:14–19 – At the foot of the mountain, a large crowd was waiting for them. A man came and knelt before Jesus and said, 'Lord, have mercy on my son. He has seizures and suffers terribly. He often falls into the fire or into the water. So, I brought him to your disciples, but they couldn't heal him.'**
>
> *Jesus said, 'You faithless and corrupt people!* **How long must I be with you? How long must I put up with you? Bring the boy here to me.' Then Jesus rebuked the demon in the boy, and it left him. From that moment the boy was well.**
>
> *Afterward the disciples asked Jesus privately, 'Why couldn't we cast out that demon?'*

Immediately after a sharp rebuke by Jesus, the disciples still thought they could approach him for help. A good leader should create an environment where their followers are not afraid to approach them even after a stern correction.

13) *Jesus welcomed all people to him irrespective of age, disability or station in society*

> **Matthew 19:13–15 – One day some parents brought their children to Jesus so he could lay his hands on them and pray for them. But the disciples scolded the parents for bothering him. But Jesus said, 'Let the children come to me. Don't stop them! For the Kingdom of Heaven belongs to those who are like these children.' And he placed his hands on their heads and blessed them before he left.**

Jesus' disciples included people from different professions, including fishermen and tax collectors. He was able to interact with people of different political persuasions.[9] He could debate intelligently with lawyers and religious leaders. As we will see in the chapter on the minor characters in the Gospel, he could relate with the sick, bereaved, rich and poor. In Matthew 19, we find he was willing and able to interact with children too. A good leader should be able to relate with the young, old, important and unimportant.

14) *Jesus gave his disciples a sense of hope*

> **Matthew 19:25–28 – The disciples were astounded. 'Then who in the world can be saved?' they asked. Jesus looked at them intently and said, 'Humanly speaking, it is impossible. But with God everything is possible.' Then Peter said to him, 'We've given up everything to follow**

---

9   Many New Testament scholars hold the view that Simon the Zealot was a member of one of the four Jewish philosophical groups of first century Judaism, namely the Zealots (Pharisees, Sadducees and Essenes – not mentioned in the New Testament – make up the other three). This group was categorised by its zeal for the one true God of Israel, an autonomous land for Israel and the belief the government at Rome was illegitimate and should be rejected. – William Telford, *The New Testament: A Beginner's Guide*, (London: Oneworld, 2014), chap. 1, Kindle.

> you. What will we get?' Jesus replied, 'I assure you that when the world is made new and the Son of Man sits upon his glorious throne, you who have been my followers will also sit on twelve thrones, judging the twelve tribes of Israel. And everyone who has given up houses or brothers or sisters or father or mother or children or property, for my sake, will receive a hundred times as much in return and will inherit eternal life. But many who are the greatest now will be least important then, and those who seem least important now will be the greatest then.'

When his disciples were discouraged or disappointed, Jesus knew what to say to stir up hope in a better future ahead. Good leaders must be able to encourage their followers in the midst of dejection and disappointment.

15) *The disciples saw Jesus as a foundation of wisdom and knowledge that they did not have*

> **Matthew 24:1-3** – As Jesus was leaving the Temple grounds, his disciples pointed out to him the various Temple buildings. But he responded, 'Do you see all these buildings? I tell you the truth, they will be completely demolished. Not one stone will be left on top of another!' Later, Jesus sat on the Mount of Olives. His disciples came to him privately and said, 'Tell us, when will all this happen? What sign will signal your return and the end of the world?'

Many leaders demand and expect their followers to come to them for advice. But ultimately that can only happen naturally if your followers think you have more knowledge than they do. The disciples thought that of Jesus and often asked him impromptu questions. In their eyes, Jesus provided clarity and extra wisdom on all topics, whether it be prayer, miracles or the future. Jesus was their go-to walking encyclopaedia.

16) The disciples sometimes misunderstood Jesus' teachings and methods

> **Matthew 26:6–13 – Meanwhile, Jesus was in Bethany at the home of Simon, a man who had previously had leprosy. While he was eating, a woman came in with a beautiful alabaster jar of expensive perfume and poured it over his head. The disciples were indignant when they saw this. 'What a waste!' they said. 'It could have been sold for a high price and the money given to the poor.' But Jesus, aware of this, replied, 'Why criticize this woman for doing such a good thing to me? You will always have the poor among you, but you will not always have me. She has poured this perfume on me to prepare my body for burial. I tell you the truth, wherever the Good News is preached throughout the world, this woman's deed will be remembered and discussed.'**

Although the disciples had the best intentions, they misunderstood Jesus' teachings and methods. Rather than look at the individual in front of them (the woman), they were concerned with the general principles of his teachings. Perhaps as they were sitting in the house of Simon the Leper, they remembered Jesus had previously taught them that perfection can be attained by giving to the poor.

> **Matthew 19:21 – Jesus told him, 'If you want to be perfect, go and sell all your possessions and give the money to the poor, and you will have treasure in heaven. Then come, follow me.'**

To correct their misunderstanding, Jesus got them to focus on the fact this was a one-off opportunity for the woman. Not only was it a special moment for her, they were reminded he would not be with them for much longer.

> **Matthew 26:10–13 – But Jesus, aware of this, replied, 'Why criticize this woman for doing such a good thing to me? You will always have the**

> poor among you, but *you will not always have me*. She has poured this perfume on me *to prepare my body for burial*. I tell you the truth, wherever the Good News is preached throughout the world, this woman's deed will be remembered and discussed.'

This was not the first time, nor was it last, that the disciples misunderstood Jesus. In Matthew 19, the disciples scolded parents for wanting Jesus to pray for their children. Again, Jesus had to correct his disciples' thinking.

> Matthew 19:13–15 – One day some parents brought their children to Jesus so he could lay his hands on them and pray for them. But the disciples scolded the parents for bothering him. But Jesus said, 'Let the children come to me. Don't stop them! For the Kingdom of Heaven belongs to those who are like these children.' And he placed his hands on their heads and blessed them before he left.

In the Garden of Gethsemane, just as Jesus was about to be arrested, one of his disciples had drawn his sword and cut off someone's ear. Again, Jesus corrected their actions and way of thinking.

> Matthew 26:50–54 – Jesus said, 'My friend, go ahead and do what you have come for.' Then the others grabbed Jesus and arrested him. But one of the men with Jesus pulled out his sword and struck the high priest's slave, slashing off his ear. 'Put away your sword,' Jesus told him. 'Those who use the sword will die by the sword. Don't you realize that I could ask my Father for thousands of angels to protect us, and he would send them instantly? But if I did, how would the Scriptures be fulfilled that describe what must happen now?'

It is the leader's responsibility to keep their followers in check. Your followers may do things to protect you and have the best intentions, but these things may lead to bad habits and have negative consequences. It is the leader's job to teach and correct them where necessary, to change mindsets and prevent the condoning of bad behaviour.

Correction also solves the problem of setting precedents which will be followed in the absence of the leader. Although repetitive, Jesus' constant pruning and correction of the disciples meant that by the time he left them, they were proper and correct representations of him.

> **Acts 4:13 – The members of the council were amazed when they saw the boldness of Peter and John, for they could see that they were ordinary men with no special training in the Scriptures. They also recognized them as men who had been with Jesus.**

17) The disciples served Jesus willingly

> **Matthew 26:17 – On the first day of the Festival of Unleavened Bread, the disciples came to Jesus and asked, 'Where do you want us to prepare the Passover meal for you?'**

The disciples were not perfect but they were willing to attend to and serve the natural needs of Jesus. The people around a good leader should love them enough to want to serve voluntarily, without instruction or coercion.

18) A good leader has connections that extend beyond their usual circle

> **Matthew 26:17–19 – On the first day of the Festival of Unleavened Bread, the disciples came to Jesus and asked, 'Where do you want us to prepare the Passover meal for you?' 'As you go into the city,' he told them, *'you will see a certain man. Tell him, "The Teacher says: My time has come, and I will eat the Passover meal with my disciples at your house."'* So, the disciples did as Jesus told them and prepared the Passover meal there.**

When a leader gives the workforce a task to complete, they usually expect the workers to find contacts who can help them accomplish the job. However, in this passage, Jesus directs the disciples to someone outside their normal circle in another city who was able to help them with their task.

A good leader has the ability to network and develop non-superficial relationships which can be called upon when needed to assist in the work of themselves and their workers.

19) Jesus had different types of relationships with his disciples

Leaders can and should have different types of relationships with their followers. Jesus had the following relationships with his disciples:

a) Friend relationship

> **Matthew 17:9 – As they went back down the mountain, Jesus commanded them, 'Don't tell anyone what you have seen until the Son of Man has been raised from the dead.'**
>
> **Matthew 26:1–2 – When Jesus had finished saying all these things, he said to his disciples, 'As you know, Passover begins in two days, and the Son of Man will be handed over to be crucified.'**
>
> **Matthew 26:37–38 – He took Peter and Zebedee's two sons, James and John, and he became anguished and distressed. He told them, 'My soul is crushed with grief to the point of death. Stay here and keep watch with me.'**

As we have already discussed, Jesus trusted the disciples enough to share his secrets and inner feelings with them. Jesus treated them as friends. John explicitly recalls the disciples were Jesus' friends because he told them everything he knew.

> **John 15:16 – I no longer call you slaves, because a master doesn't confide in his slaves. Now you are my friends, since I have told you everything the Father told me.**

One of the striking features of Moses was the way the Lord spoke to him. The Lord spoke to Moses as a person would speak to a friend.

> **Exodus 33:11 – Inside the Tent of Meeting, *the Lord would speak to Moses face to face, as one speaks to a friend.* Afterward Moses would return to the camp, but the young man who assisted him, Joshua son of Nun, would remain behind in the Tent of Meeting.**

A leader cannot claim to be a friend to their followers or workers if they do not talk to them and do not share things with them directly.

b) Teacher–disciple relationship

The Gospel of Matthew is littered with accounts of Jesus teaching his disciples. Some of these teachings were instigated by Jesus, others by questions from the disciples. Some of the teachings were influenced by the circumstances they found themselves in as they travelled together. Other teachings were in response to the actions of people they encountered on their journeys.

The key points to notice are that Jesus was constantly teaching and interacting with his disciples. He had enough contact with them to become their source of knowledge. As a leader, you may know far more than the people you are leading, but if you have hardly any contact or interactions with them, you will never be able to teach them. The teacher–disciple relationship will never blossom.

c) Master–servant relationship

> **Matthew 26:17–19 – On the first day of the Festival of Unleavened Bread, the disciples came to Jesus and asked, *'Where do you want us to prepare the Passover meal for you?'* 'As you go into the city,' he told them, 'you will see a certain man. Tell him, "The Teacher says: My time has come, and I will eat the Passover meal with my disciples at your house."' *So, the disciples did as Jesus told them and prepared the Passover meal there.***

The disciples saw Jesus as their master whom they were happy to serve.

d) Family relationship

> **Matthew 26:20 – When it was evening, Jesus sat down at the table with the Twelve.**

Jesus shared festivities with his disciples. The Passover is traditionally an occasion for family. It is pretty much like sitting down for Christmas, Easter or Thanksgiving dinner. These events are usually shared and celebrated with family. They even sang a song of praise together.

> **Matthew 26:30 – Then they sang a hymn and went out to the Mount of Olives.**

After his resurrection, Jesus referred to his disciples as his brothers. The disciples remained his family even in his exalted state.

> **Matthew 28:10 – Then Jesus said to them, 'Don't be afraid! Go tell my brothers to leave for Galilee, and they will see me there.'**

All these relationships are possible at once and in their own right. Your followers must be comfortable enough around you to be able to switch between each relationship freely and willingly without issue or fear.

20) Jesus always spoke truth to his disciples

Matthew 28:20–21 – When it was evening, Jesus sat down at the table with the Twelve. While they were eating, he said, 'I tell you the truth, one of you will betray me.'

Jesus spoke truth to those around him irrespective of the circumstances or setting. Whether it changed the mood or not, Jesus was concerned with telling them the truth they needed to hear at that time. In all likelihood, Jesus was probably led by the Spirit to do this.

To understand the setting, we must imagine this as Christmas dinner. Picture tucking into the turkey and then a family member announcing that someone at the table will betray them. Quite frankly, everyone at the dinner table would be completely and utterly baffled. There would be an awkward silence, laughter or a question regarding the mindset of the person who had spoken.

Sometimes we are prompted to speak truth in the midst of happiness but choose to ignore that still small prompt because we do not want to be a disrupter or start an argument.

That being said, it is not always appropriate to speak so directly, especially if the people you are with do not know you. But with those close to us, it is often best to speak truth rather than remain silent. We must, however, be led by the Holy Spirit and deliver truth with grace.

John 1:17 – For the law was given through Moses; grace and truth came through Jesus Christ. (NIV)

21) *Do not be surprised if the people close to you are the ones who betray you*

> **Matthew 26:31–35 – On the way, Jesus told them, 'Tonight all of you will desert me. For the Scriptures say, "God will strike the Shepherd, and the sheep of the flock will be scattered." But after I have been raised from the dead, I will go ahead of you to Galilee and meet you there.' Peter declared, 'Even if everyone else deserts you, I will never desert you.' Jesus replied, *'I tell you the truth, Peter—this very night, before the rooster crows, you will deny three times that you even know me.'* 'No!' Peter insisted. *'Even if I have to die with you, I will never deny you!'* And all the other disciples vowed the same.**

You must know that even your closest followers can betray you. Not only can they betray you once; they may betray you on multiple occasions. At this point, it is worth remembering that if it happened to Jesus, it can definitely happen to you or me.

> **Matthew 10:24 – The disciple is not above his master, nor the servant above his lord.**

Betrayal and denial alone are not reasons to reject or disown a person. People are not always aware of themselves or what they are capable of doing. That is why we should not be moved by what people say to us. Peter probably believed in that moment he would not betray Jesus. Perhaps this is why Jesus did not press his point or seek to prove his words to him. In our toughest moments, we are likely to be alone. We must trust in God for our deliverance. Christ went into the garden knowing he would end up alone but dependent on God.

22) *Good leaders constantly check on the state and well-being of their followers*

> **Matthew 26:40 – Then *he returned to the disciples* and found them asleep. He said to Peter, 'Couldn't you watch with me even one hour?'**

> **Matthew 26:43 – When *he returned to them again*, he found them sleeping, for they couldn't keep their eyes open.**

A good leader repeatedly checks on the state of his or her people. Jesus went to pray for himself, for his road ahead. Despite this, he stopped what he was doing to check on his disciples. He did not forget about the people he was with, even though he had his own objective. He checked on them not once, but twice.

23) *Jesus accepted the weaknesses of his disciples*

> **Matthew 26:43–45 – When he returned to them again, he found them sleeping, for they couldn't keep their eyes open. So, he went to pray a third time, saying the same things again. Then he came to the disciples and said, *'Go ahead and sleep. Have your rest.* But look—the time has come. The Son of Man is betrayed into the hands of sinners.'**

Having checked on his disciples, Jesus saw they couldn't do what he was doing. The first time he checked on them he gave them a teaching, but this did not solve the problem.

> **Matthew 26:40–41 – Then he returned to the disciples and found them asleep. He said to Peter, 'Couldn't you watch with me even one hour? Keep watch and pray, so that you will not give in to temptation. For the spirit is willing, but the body is weak!'**

On the second occasion, he did not rebuke them but accepted them as they were and even told them to sleep on.

> **Matthew 26:45 – Then he came to the disciples and said, 'Go ahead and sleep. Have your rest.'**

A leader will sometimes see that the followers cannot do what the leader is able to do, no matter how hard they are pushed. The disciples could not physically stay awake. It was beyond them; they could not keep their eyes open.

> **Matthew 26:43 – When he returned to them again, he found them sleeping, for they couldn't keep their eyes open.**

A leader must be willing to see the weaknesses of his followers without judgement.

24) A good leader must be flexible and adaptable

> **Matthew 26:45–46 – Then he came to the disciples and said, 'Go ahead and sleep. Have your rest. But look—the time has come. The Son of Man is betrayed into the hands of sinners. Up, let's be going. Look, my betrayer is here!'**

A good leader is adaptable. Jesus had accepted the state of the disciples and told them to rest. When he saw Judas had arrived sooner than expected, his plan changed. Good leaders need to be flexible. They should never allow their enemy to see them caught off guard. Good leaders should be ready to go and to encourage those they are with to change course.

25) A good leader must be constant and authentic even when under pressure

> **Matthew 26:57-58 – Then the people who had arrested Jesus led him to the home of Caiaphas, the high priest, where the teachers of religious law and the elders had gathered. Meanwhile, Peter followed him at a distance and came to the high priest's courtyard. He went in and sat with the guards and waited to see how it would all end.**

After Jesus' arrest, Peter followed behind and watched the whole trial. Good leaders must remain authentic at all times because they do not know when their followers are watching or what they are learning from them.

26) Jesus did not forget about his disciples after his resurrection

> **Matthew 28:10 – Then Jesus said to them, 'Don't be afraid! Go tell my brothers to leave for Galilee, and they will see me there.'**

After Jesus was resurrected, his first thought was for his disciples. Jesus did not forget the people who had been with him when he was nothing. Despite their mistakes, he remembered that for the most part they had been with him, supported him and travelled with him. They remained his family even after he was exalted.

This may seem like a trivial point, but the truth is Jesus could have appeared to anyone – Pilate, Herod, the religious leaders, any of the people he had healed or any random guy on the street, but he chose his disciples. The point to note here is that we should not forget the people who have helped us when we finally see the vision come to pass. Perhaps a good modern example of this comes from the tech world – many of the people who started and helped build Facebook, Amazon, Google and the like became multimillionaires when these firms started trading publicly. When the rewards were distributed, they were not forgotten.

27) *Do not be discouraged if people still doubt you after your dream has been realised*

> **Matthew 28:17-20 – When they saw him, they worshiped him—but some of them doubted! Jesus came and told his disciples, 'I have been given all authority in heaven and on earth. Therefore, go and make disciples of all the nations, baptizing them in the name of the Father and the Son and the Holy Spirit. Teach these new disciples to obey all the commands I have given you. And be sure of this: I am with you always, even to the end of the age.'**

Even after the vision has been made real, some people will still doubt you. Not everyone who follows you will believe in you initially. It was after the Holy Spirit descended that all disciples believed in the resurrection.

Do not disregard people prematurely because of doubt. Some will not believe completely until later on in the story. Despite the doubt of some of the disciples, Jesus still commissioned all to go into the world. Christian tradition purports that the disciple most known for doubting Jesus' resurrection, Thomas, made it as far as India as a missionary!

CHAPTER 4

JESUS' INTERACTIONS WITH JUDAS

Perhaps one of the most interesting relationships in the Gospels is the relationship between Jesus and Judas. The role Judas played in Jesus' death often overshadows the dynamics of this relationship. It is quite possible that 2,000 years of commentary has blurred the nuances of this relationship. This chapter seeks to understand what can be learnt from the interactions between Jesus and Judas.

1) *Jesus chose Judas to be one of the twelve disciples*

> **Matthew 10:1–4 – And when *he had called unto him his twelve disciples*, he gave them power against unclean spirits, to cast them out, and to heal all manner of sickness and all manner of disease. Now the names of the twelve apostles are these; ... and *Judas Iscariot, who also betrayed him*. (KJV)**

Like all the other disciples, Judas was given the power to heal the sick. He was sent out with the rest to preach the message of repentance.

> **Matthew 10:5 – These twelve Jesus sent forth, and commanded them, saying ... (KJV)**

It is not clear from the Gospel of Matthew when exactly Jesus knew Judas would betray him. Had he known from the beginning of his ministry then it is important to note he did not treat Judas any differently from the other disciples. The natural response would have been to keep Judas at arm's length but, for whatever reason, Jesus did not do this.

2) *Jesus spoke truth to Judas*

> **Matthew 26:25–26 – Then Judas, which betrayed him, answered and said, Master, is it I? He said unto him, 'Thou hast said.' And as they were eating, Jesus took bread, and blessed it, and brake it, and gave it to the disciples, and said, 'Take, eat; this is my body.' (KJV)**

When Judas asked Jesus if he was the one to betray him, Jesus replied with the truth. The disciples were at table in the middle of their annual Passover meal, but Jesus was still able to speak the truth while they were eating. To put this into some context in our modern world, many of us have special meals on Good Friday or Easter Sunday; it is in this context that we should view this discussion. Imagine answering a question about betrayal and deceit over Christmas dinner! Ordinarily, to maintain the atmosphere, we might deflect the question, answer with a partial truth, change the subject or ignore the question altogether. But that was not Jesus; in the midst of the celebration, he was able to speak the truth to his friend, mentee, student and companion.

We must remember that, despite the betrayal, the Bible does not teach us that Jesus rejected Judas. It was Judas who was not able to recover from his actions. At this stage, Judas was still being treated as one of the twelve.

Perhaps this ability to speak the truth and continue as normal is testament to Christ's forgiving nature. By this time, it is clear Jesus knew what Judas was about to do. But he was able to relate to Judas as normal, so much so that the other disciples did not notice what had just happened.

As leaders, we should be able to speak the truth to those around us, irrespective of the circumstances. That being said, our truth does not need to be confrontational. While Jesus told Judas the truth, it was in such a way that no one else seemed to notice. It did not impact on or change the atmosphere. After such a frank discussion, they all continued eating. Nothing changed at all. The other disciples did not react in any way. We can only assume they understood the significance of the conversation between Jesus and Judas later, after the events of the succeeding days.

Good leaders have the ability to correct their followers in such a way that those in the vicinity are unaware of what is happening. This type of correction provides space for the offender to change, if willing. It allows for a U-turn, as there is no confrontation or trial before the event. Even if the perpetrator follows through with their actions, there is still space for recovery. We know this to be true because Jesus used the same approach with Peter.

> **Matthew 26:33-34 – Peter answered and said unto him, 'Though all men shall be offended because of thee, yet will I never be offended.' Jesus said unto him, 'Verily I say unto thee, that this night, before the cock crow, thou shalt deny me thrice.' (KJV)**

3) *Jesus was never caught off guard nor surprised by Judas' actions*

> **Matthew 26:46-47 – 'Rise, let us be going: behold, he is at hand that doth betray me.' And while he yet spake, lo, Judas, one of the twelve, came, and with him a great multitude with swords and staves, from the chief priests and elders of the people. (KJV)**

Jesus was ready for the betrayal and did not appear surprised or shocked when Judas arrived with a crowd of people with weapons. Often, we are caught off guard by the enemy because we are not expecting such a large attack. We must learn to be alert to enemy attacks even if they are disproportionate to our expectations. The aim of the enemy is to prevent us from walking in the promise and call of God.

> **John 10:10 – The thief does not come except to steal, and to kill, and to destroy. (NKJV)**

We should be attentive to this and understand that he will do whatever it takes to destabilise us, no matter how much strength is required to do so. Despite the overwhelming force of the group which came to arrest Jesus, he remained calm and unflustered. The crowd and weapons did not cause him to become reactionary. As leaders, we must learn to surprise the enemy by remaining alert but calm in the midst of chaos.

4) *Jesus called Judas 'Friend' at the moment of betrayal*

> **Matthew 26:50 – And Jesus said unto him, 'Friend, wherefore art thou come?' Then came they, and laid hands on Jesus, and took him. (KJV)**

One of the most difficult things to recover from is betrayal by a close friend. But here we see that, contrary to human nature, Jesus referred to Judas as his friend during the actual act of betrayal. He still held on to the relationship despite the circumstances. In this moment, we see that betrayal is not necessarily a reason to disregard or give up on a relationship.

The use of the word 'friend' here is sometimes taken to be a simple greeting, and is therefore disregarded. But if we look more broadly at when Jesus spoke, we find that every word he uttered had purpose and direction. There were no accidental or casual words with unclear meanings. He spoke directly and with authority.

> **Matthew 7:29 – For he taught them as one having authority, and not as the scribes. (KJV)**

> **John 6:63 – ... the words that I speak unto you, they are spirit, and they are life. (KJV)**

He spoke to the fig tree and it withered.

> **Matthew 21:19 – And when he saw a fig tree in the way, he came to it, and found nothing thereon, but leaves only, and said unto it, 'Let no fruit grow on thee henceforward for ever.' And presently the fig tree withered away. (KJV)**

He was not afraid to call people out if required. He called one of his closest and most trusted disciples Satan and told the Pharisees they were behaving like their father, the devil.

> **Matthew 16:23 – But he turned, and said unto Peter, 'Get thee behind me, Satan: thou art an offence unto me: for thou savourest not the things that be of God, but those that be of men.' (KJV)**

> **John 8:44 – 'Ye are of your father the devil, and the lusts of your father ye will do.' (KJV)**

Thus, when we see the word 'friend' in Matthew 26:50, we ought to take it to mean what it does mean; namely that Jesus still regarded Judas as a friend.

One of the fundamental tenets of Jesus' teachings is forgiveness.

> Matthew 6:12 – And forgive us our debts, as we forgive our debtors. (KJV)

> Matthew 18:21–22 – Then came Peter to him, and said, 'Lord, how oft shall my brother sin against me, and I forgive him? till seven times?' Jesus saith unto him, 'I say not unto thee, until seven times: but, until seventy times seven.' (KJV)

Ultimately, in forgiving Judas so quickly and without hesitation, Jesus was merely practising what he had preached. But when one examines Judas' character a bit further, perhaps Jesus' response was due to his relationship with and knowledge of Judas.

Unlike Absalom or Lucifer, Judas did not have (as far as we can tell) a long-standing plan to overthrow Jesus.

> Isaiah 14:12–14 – How art thou fallen from heaven, O Lucifer, son of the morning! How art thou cut down to the ground, which didst weaken the nations! For *thou hast said in thine heart*, I will ascend into heaven, I will exalt my throne above the stars of God: I will sit also upon the mount of the congregation, in the sides of the north. I will ascend above the heights of the clouds; *I will be like the most High*. (KJV)

Judas did not openly oppose Jesus' leadership. Neither did he try to convert any of the other disciples to his way of thinking.

> 2 Samuel 15:1–6 – And it came to pass after this, that Absalom prepared him chariots and horses, and fifty men to run before him. And Absalom rose up early, and stood beside the way of the gate: and it was so, that when any man that had a controversy came to the king for judgment, then Absalom called unto him, and said, 'Of what city art thou?' And he said, 'Thy servant is of one of the tribes of Israel.' And Absalom said unto him, 'See, thy matters are good and right; but there is no man deputed of the king to hear thee.' Absalom said moreover, 'Oh that I

> were made judge in the land, that every man which hath any suit or cause might come unto me, and I would do him justice!' And it was so, that when any man came nigh to him to do him obeisance, he put forth his hand, and took him, and kissed him. And on this manner did Absalom to all Israel that came to the king for judgment: so, *Absalom stole the hearts of the men of Israel.* (KJV)

What led Judas to betray Jesus was his love for money. Judas was tempted and attracted to the offer of money by the chief priests.

> Matthew 26:14–16 – Then one of the twelve, called Judas Iscariot, went unto the chief priests. And said unto them, 'What will ye give me, and I will deliver him unto you?' And they covenanted with him for thirty pieces of silver. And from that time he sought opportunity to betray him. (KJV)

Paul teaches us that the love of money is the root of all evil. It is no wonder that Judas betrayed Jesus!

> 1 Timothy 6:10 – For the love of money is the root of all evil: which while some coveted after, they have erred from the faith, and pierced themselves through with many sorrows. (KJV)

Perhaps Jesus still referred to him as friend knowing Judas had only succumbed to a weakness – his love for money – that he was unable to overcome. Perhaps Jesus knew Judas was unaware of the gravity of what he had done. Judas, at that stage, could never have known that throughout history he would be remembered as the betrayer of the Son of God. Perhaps Jesus knew Judas did not inherently dislike him or that he was not out to overthrow his leadership. Perhaps Jesus knew Judas would find it difficult to recover from his actions when it finally dawned on him what he had done for money.

> **Matthew 27:3–5** – Then Judas, which had betrayed him, when he saw that he was condemned, repented himself, and brought again the thirty pieces of silver to the chief priests and elders, Saying, 'I have sinned in that I have betrayed the innocent blood.' And they said, 'What is that to us? see thou to that.' And he cast down the pieces of silver in the temple, and departed, and went and hanged himself. (KJV)

All of these factors may have influenced Jesus' response to Judas.

What does this mean for us as leaders? It suggests that before discarding or ending a relationship with someone because of betrayal we ought to examine the person and the reasons for the betrayal. In addition to forgiving those who have hurt us, we should also ask ourselves – did this person do this because they were facing a difficulty? Is there a weakness this person is yet to overcome? Am I willing to accept this weakness and guide them through it?

CHAPTER 5

JESUS' INTERATIONS WITH MINOR CHARACTERS

Throughout the Gospel, Matthew recounts the various encounters Jesus had with different people. Each encounter reveals something more about the personality and character of Jesus. Each encounter reveals further his ability to relate and interact with people from across society. Apart from the lessons to be learnt from Jesus, there are also lessons to be learnt from the minor characters who in many instances received the vision or dream they had been expecting from God. In this chapter we will look at each interaction and see what can be gleaned from it.

1) The crowd

    a) Jesus withdrew from the crowd to be with his disciples

    Matthew 8:18 – When *Jesus saw the crowd* around him, he instructed his disciples to *cross to the other side of the lake*.

There must come a time when we intentionally withdraw from the crowd. As leaders, we must find time to separate ourselves from the noise of the crowd. It does not mean that we are to reject the crowd entirely – after all, Jesus interacted and spoke to the crowd more than he withdrew from it. Therefore, there will be times when we must disengage from the crowd. For many of us today, this may not be a literal crowd, but may be a social media crowd. Some of us may need to learn how to retreat from the crowd on Twitter, Instagram, Facebook and WhatsApp.

Surprisingly, in this passage, Jesus did not withdraw from the crowd to be alone or to pray to the Father but, rather, to interact with his disciples.

> **Matthew 8:19–23 – Then** *one of the teachers of religious law* **said to him, 'Teacher, I will follow you wherever you go.' But Jesus replied, 'Foxes have dens to live in, and birds have nests, but the Son of Man has no place even to lay his head.'** *Another of his disciples* **said, 'Lord, first let me return home and bury my father.' But Jesus told him, 'Follow me now. Let the spiritually dead bury their own dead.' Then Jesus got into the boat and started across the lake with** *his disciples.*

Leaders must be in the habit of withdrawing from the crowd to be with those with whom they are working. Jesus did this more than once.

> **Matthew 20:17 – As Jesus was going up to Jerusalem, he took the** *twelve disciples aside privately* **and told them what was going to happen to him.**

Leaders must invest more in the people around them than in the crowd. Leaders must realise if they are able to develop and build up their followers, they will have a greater impact than just relating with the general crowd.

b) Jesus helped those who followed him

> **Matthew 19:2 – Large crowds followed him there, and he healed their sick.**

It sounds intuitive and obvious but it is worth stating explicitly – people follow a leader whom they think can help them or solve their problems. Jesus was able to solve the problems of the people who followed him. For those he was unable to relate to directly, the stories of those he had previously helped persuaded them to follow him, in the hope they too would be helped.

2) *The teacher of the law and the scribe*

> **Matthew 8:18–22 – When Jesus saw the crowd around him, he instructed his disciples to cross to the other side of the lake. Then *one of the teachers of religious law* said to him, 'Teacher, I will follow you wherever you go.' But Jesus replied, 'Foxes have dens to live in, and birds have nests, but the Son of Man has no place even to lay his head.' Another of his disciples said, 'Lord, first let me return home and bury my father.' But Jesus told him, 'Follow me now. Let the spiritually dead bury their own dead.'**

a) Jesus knew and understood each of his disciples individually

The first thing to note here is that Jesus was trying to separate himself from the crowd but allowed a group to follow him. We can imagine him trying to make his way to the boat and perhaps allowing a small group to continue walking with him as he made his way. Or perhaps he stopped to hear the questions from these two disciples.

The first teacher of the law then claims he will follow Jesus wherever he goes, possibly implying he would like to be included in the group that got into the boat and went with Jesus. In response, Jesus explains to him that where he is going is undefined. He has no fixed abode.

> **Matthew 8:19-20 – Then one of the teachers of religious law said to him, 'Teacher, I will follow you wherever you go.' But Jesus replied, 'Foxes have dens to live in, and birds have nests, but** *the Son of Man has no place even to lay his head.***'**

To be clear, this was not meant to be a deterrent to the teacher, but was in fact a statement of fact. Jesus must have known him well enough (whether by personal interaction or spiritual discernment) to know the lack of stability would have been an issue for the man. Jesus was simply reminding him of what it means to follow him.

Another disciple who was following heard the discussion and was not deterred by the lack of certainty. His issue was that he wanted Jesus to wait for him while he sorted his life out.

> **Matthew 8:21-22 – Another of his disciples said, '***Lord, first let me return home and bury my father.***' But Jesus told him, 'Follow me now. Let the spiritually dead bury their own dead.'**

To this disciple, rather than explain the difficulties of following him, Jesus told him to drop what he was doing and follow immediately. In other words, Jesus gave two different pieces of advice to two different people who wanted to do the same thing. Leaders must know the people who are following them so they can advise and help them according to their individual situations. Good leaders must know that blanket instructions do not always help their followers.

Separately, as leaders, we must constantly ask ourselves, what is the Lord specifically saying to me in this situation? What may apply to the person down the road or sitting near us at church may not apply to us specifically.

3) The ruler

> **Matthew 9:18-19 – While he spake these things unto them, behold, there came a certain ruler, and worshipped him, saying, 'My daughter is even now dead: but come and lay thy hand upon her, and she shall live.' And Jesus arose, and followed him, and so did his disciples. (KJV)**

   a) The ruler approached and worshipped Jesus despite the circumstances

   > **Matthew 9:18 – While he spake these things unto them, behold, there *came* a certain ruler, and *worshipped* him, (KJV)**

For the ruler to receive his miracle, he first took the step of approaching Jesus. For many of us, approaching God in the midst of death *feels* and *is* difficult. But we must remember that in going to him, we will receive our healing and help. Hebrews reminds us we are able to do this because Jesus understands our pain and weaknesses.

> **Hebrews 4:15–16 – This High Priest of ours understands our weaknesses, for he faced all of the same testings we do, yet he did not sin. So let us come boldly to the throne of our gracious God. There we will receive his mercy, and we will find grace to help us when we need it most.**

   b) Worshipping and acknowledging God does not mean we do not have any problems, nor does it mean we cannot talk about our problems

   > **Matthew 9:18 – While he spake these things unto them, behold, there came a certain ruler, and worshipped him, saying, 'My daughter is even now dead: but come and lay thy hand upon her, and she shall live.' (KJV)**

The ruler was not only able to worship Jesus, but he also brought his problem to him directly. We can acknowledge God for who he is and at the same time tell him about our deepest and most pressing issues.

c) The Lord will respond to our problems

Matthew 9:19 – So Jesus and his disciples got up and went with him.

At his weakest, Jesus responded to the ruler's request. There was no discussion or question, just action. Not only did Jesus follow the man to help him, he took his disciples with him. We must remember that when we pray, the Lord responds.

d) In the same way Jesus responded to the ruler's problem, good leaders should respond to the needs and requests of their followers

Good leaders should be concerned with their followers' problems. In some instances, we should stop what we are doing and give our full attention to the needs of those following us. Not only should we stop what we are doing, in some extreme cases all those working with us should stop and turn their attention to the needs of the person with the problem. This level of attention reveals to the person they are not only important but valued and loved. Such love can only lead to undivided loyalty. I believe that, in addition to the miracles Jesus performed, the crowds that followed were attracted and impressed by his love for individuals. Not only would the people he met have felt special and wanted, but their friends, families and wider community would have been impressed by him too. Their only response to this level of love would have been to tell others about it. People respond well to interest and love.

Good leaders should make it their aim to respond to the needs of the people with whom they are working, with speed and urgency.

> e) People will laugh at you and mock you
>
> **Matthew 9:23-24 – When Jesus arrived at the official's home, he saw the noisy crowd and heard the funeral music. 'Get out!' he told them. 'The girl isn't dead; she's only asleep.'** *But the crowd laughed at him.*

We should never be shocked or surprised when people respond to our faith with laughter – whether it be our faith in God generally or if we believe in God for something which seems and looks impossible. Remember, the servant is not greater than the master! If people laughed at Jesus, they will certainly laugh at you!

Our response to mockers should be the same as Jesus' – we should tell them to *get out*!

The book of Proverbs teaches us the same thing:

> **Proverbs 22:10 –** *Throw out the mocker,* **and fighting goes, too. Quarrels and** *insults will disappear.*

We should not be afraid to move people along if they are preventing us from believing in the vision that God has given us. Laughter and mockers discourage us and reduce our faith levels. This can be detrimental to our progress because we know it is our faith that activates our blessings and moves the hand of God.

Perhaps Jesus was working by this principle when he sent the crowd packing. It was only after the crowd left the room that he began to work the miracle.

> **Matthew 9:25** – After the crowd was put outside, however, Jesus went in and took the girl by the hand, and she stood up!

4) *The woman with the issue of blood*

> **Matthew 9:20–22** – Just then a woman who had suffered for twelve years with constant bleeding came up behind him. She touched the fringe of his robe, for she thought, 'If I can just touch his robe, I will be healed.' Jesus turned around, and when he saw her he said, 'Daughter, be encouraged! Your faith has made you well.' And the woman was healed at that moment.

a) The Lord knows our innermost thoughts, but we must act to receive our healing

The woman with the issue of blood did not have to utter a word for Jesus to respond to her. We know there is power in prayer and, if we ask, things will be given to us.

> **Matthew 7:7** – Ask, and it shall be given you; seek, and ye shall find; knock, and it shall be opened unto you. (KJV)

But here we see there are instances where words are not needed for God to respond. The woman only thought about her healing and acted on her thoughts. Her thoughts plus the action were deemed enough for healing and wholeness. Her belief led to action which led to healing.

> **Matthew 9:22** – 'Daughter, be encouraged! Your faith has made you well.' And the woman was healed at that moment.

We must remember it was both her thought and her action of touching which led to her healing. Without action, our faith is dead.

> **James 2:26 – For as the body without the spirit is dead, so faith without works is dead also. (KJV)**

   b) Jesus had the ability to give attention to more than one person at the same time – he could multitask

The healing of the woman with the issue of blood happened on the way to the ruler's house. In the preceding verse, Jesus follows the ruler to his house, and in the succeeding verse he arrives at the house.

> **Matthew 9:19 – And Jesus arose, and followed him, and so did his disciples. (KJV)**

> **Matthew 9:23 – And when Jesus came into the ruler's house … (KJV)**

A good leader must have the ability to deal with different people at the same time. A good leader has the ability to give the specific attention required to solve or assist the needs of their followers. Jesus did not say to the woman – *'Hold on, be right back. I am sorting out something else.'* He addressed her issue on the way to solving someone else's problem. It is essential that a good leader develops the art of multitasking, handling and managing many different issues at the same time. Because of this ability, neither the ruler nor the woman felt insignificant or unwanted. It is therefore critical for leaders to expand this skill if they want to maintain the happiness of the people who follow them.

5) The disciples of John the Baptist

> **Matthew 11:2-6 – John the Baptist, who was in prison, heard about all the things the Messiah was doing. So he sent his disciples to ask Jesus, 'Are you the Messiah we've been expecting, or should we keep looking for someone else?'**

> Jesus told them, 'Go back to John and tell him what you have heard and seen— the blind see, the lame walk, those with leprosy are cured, the deaf hear, the dead are raised to life, and the Good News is being preached to the poor.' And he added, 'God blesses those who do not fall away because of me.'

a) Actions usually speak louder than words

Rather than provide a theological answer or topical debate to the question from John's disciples, Jesus replied by telling them about what he had been doing. Sometimes, to answer the questions of enquiring minds or doubters, it is better just to show or tell them what you have done. Often, people are satisfied if you simply bring their attention to what you have *actually* done rather than what they might *think* you have done or what they have *heard* you have done.

People may be unsure of following someone because they are unsure of their background or have heard negative stories. But, if you can point them to tangible actions, minds can be changed in your favour. If people can see your fruit, they will know you and then follow you.

> Matthew 7:17–20 – A good tree produces good fruit, and a bad tree produces bad fruit. A good tree can't produce bad fruit, and a bad tree can't produce good fruit. So every tree that does not produce good fruit is chopped down and thrown into the fire. Yes, just as you can identify a tree by its fruit, so you can identify people by their actions.

6) The rich man

> Matthew 19:16–22 – Someone came to Jesus with this question: 'Teacher, what good deed must I do to have eternal life?' *'Why ask me about what is good?'* Jesus replied. *'There is only One who is good. But to answer your question—if you want to receive eternal life, keep*

the commandments.' 'Which ones?' the man asked. And Jesus replied: 'You must not murder. You must not commit adultery. You must not steal. You must not testify falsely. Honor your father and mother. Love your neighbor as yourself.' 'I've obeyed all these commandments,' the young man replied. 'What else must I do?' Jesus told him, 'If you want to be perfect, go and sell all your possessions and give the money to the poor, and you will have treasure in heaven. Then come, follow me.' But when the young man heard this, he went away sad, for he had many possessions.

a) Goodness is often unattainable and can be a distraction

As leaders, many of us often strive for complete excellence on every level. This pursuit can often cause us to lose sight of our ultimate vision. There is no harm in setting a good standard. People only follow what they aspire to be or something that looks worth following. But we must be careful not to get side-tracked by trying to perfect a small task at the detriment of the greater goal – the reason being that we are unlikely to reach the level of perfection we are looking for because, ultimately, only God is good.

I remember proofreading essays multiple times before deadlines at university, only to find an error *after* submitting the piece of work. I then decided one day I would stop rereading my essays after submission because they were never going to be perfect. There was no point in getting frustrated over human error. That is the point we have to remember – we are humans and therefore prone to error, not perfect. If we remember this, we will not hold ourselves to a standard we cannot meet and neither will we hold others to a standard they cannot meet. This simple truth may prevent us from dismissing helpers or workers prematurely because of their inability to reach our unattainable standards of perfection.

b) Not everyone who wants to follow you is willing to do what it takes to work with or follow you

> **Matthew 19:20–22 – 'I've obeyed all these commandments,' the young man replied. 'What else must I do?' Jesus told him, 'If you want to be perfect, go and sell all your possessions and give the money to the poor, and you will have treasure in heaven. Then come, follow me.' But when the young man heard this, he went away sad, for he had many possessions.**

Despite being able to obey the commandments, the rich man was unable to sell all he had, give the money to the poor and follow Jesus. This did not lead Jesus to change his standards, nor did he condemn or reject the man; it was the man who changed his mind and left. It is worth noting here the man was sad he could not follow Jesus – just because someone does not give up what they are doing to follow you does not mean they don't care about you or your vision. It simply means they view what they have to give up as too great a price to pay. Yet this does not mean the price in itself is too high; there will be people who are willing to give up what they have to follow you and help you pursue your vision or call.

We see in the following verses the disciples were able to do what this man couldn't do.

> **Matthew 19:27 – Then Peter said to him, 'We've given up everything to follow you. What will we get?'**

This tells us there will be people who are willing to follow us despite the fact there will also be people who will leave us. We should therefore not be pressured to lower our requirements if some people *do* leave us.

7) The blind men

> **Matthew 20:29-34** – As Jesus and the disciples left the town of Jericho, a large crowd followed behind. Two blind men were sitting beside the road. When they heard that Jesus was coming that way, they began shouting, 'Lord, Son of David, have mercy on us!' 'Be quiet!' the crowd yelled at them. But they only shouted louder, 'Lord, Son of David, have mercy on us!' When Jesus heard them, he stopped and called, 'What do you want me to do for you?' 'Lord,' they said, 'we want to see!' Jesus felt sorry for them and touched their eyes. Instantly they could see! Then they followed him.

a) Don't be surprised if people try to silence you!

Whether it be directly or indirectly, on social media or in person, in all likelihood people will try to silence you. This could happen by dismissing your dream or making you feel your opinion doesn't count. The correct response to this is to ignore the noise of the crowd and pursue your vision even harder than before. The blind men shouted louder than before, until they caught Jesus' attention.

> **Matthew 20:31** – 'Be quiet!' the crowd yelled at them. *But they only shouted louder, 'Lord, Son of David, have mercy on us!'*

I am not saying you should shout louder and engage in topical debates on social media. Paul taught Timothy to avoid foolish and useless debates.

> **1 Timothy 6:20** – Timothy, guard what God has entrusted to you. Avoid godless, foolish discussions with those who oppose you with their so-called knowledge.

I am saying these voices should not distract or discourage you from what you are doing or what you believe to be your God-given assignment.

The blind men ignored the crowd and were rewarded with healing in the subsequent verses.

> Matthew 20:34 – Jesus felt sorry for them and touched their eyes. *Instantly they could see!* Then they followed him.

b) Continue to cry out to God in prayer until you see the results you are looking for

The loudness of the cries of the blind men caused Jesus to turn around, acknowledge them, call them over, have compassion on them and answer their request.

> Matthew 20:31–34 – But they only shouted louder, 'Lord, Son of David, have mercy on us!' When Jesus heard them, he stopped and called, 'What do you want me to do for you?' 'Lord,' they said, 'we want to see!' *Jesus felt sorry for them* and touched their eyes. Instantly they could see! Then they followed him.

As Christian leaders, we ought never to get tired of praying. Our mantra should be that we will Pray Until Something Happens (PUSH). Jesus taught us the power of persistence in prayer in a parable in Luke.

> Luke 18:1–8 – One day Jesus told his disciples a story to show that they should *always pray and never give up.* 'There was a judge in a certain city,' he said, 'who neither feared God nor cared about people. A widow of that city came to him repeatedly, saying, "Give me justice in this dispute with my enemy." The judge ignored her for a while, but finally he said to himself, "I don't fear God or care about people, but this woman is driving me crazy. I'm going to see that she gets justice, because she is wearing me out with her constant requests!"'
>
> Then the Lord said, 'Learn a lesson from this unjust judge. Even he rendered a just decision in the end. So don't you think God will surely

give justice to his chosen people who cry out to him day and night? Will he keep putting them off? I tell you, he will grant justice to them quickly! But when the Son of Man returns, how many will he find on the earth who have faith?'

Whenever I read this passage I am constantly reminded and challenged to continue in prayer because my answer *will* come; the question is, will I still be there to receive it when it finally shows up? Many times, we throw in the towel just before we are about to be delivered or the dream is fulfilled.

We must remember persistence brings results, in the natural and also in the physical. If you regularly go to the gym and exercise, you will lose weight. But you must be patient to see the fruits of your labour. Rapid weight loss is not advised and can often lead to other health issues or quickly regaining weight. Perhaps this is the same with prayer. Perhaps God does not give us instant answers because he knows it may be bad for our spiritual health or it may take us back to our unsaved nature. We must therefore believe and trust in his sovereignty and timing, holding on to the fact all things work for our good.

> **Romans 8:28 – And we know that God causes everything to work together for the good of those who love God and are called according to his purpose for them.**

c) Give attention to people who are striving to get your attention

Usually, as leaders, we are engrossed in what we are doing and often do not take the time to stop and notice those who are trying to get our attention. Jesus did the exact opposite here and gained two followers.

> **Matthew 20:34 – Jesus felt sorry for them and touched their eyes. Instantly they could see!** *Then they followed him.*

By stopping and helping these blind men, his following and influence increased. Sometimes it is worth stopping to hear what those who need us to help them actually want from us. We may never know who or what we are ignoring; disregarding people may turn out to work against us.

8) Simon the leper

> **Matthew 26:6–9 – Meanwhile, Jesus was in Bethany at the home of Simon, a man who had previously had leprosy. While he was eating, a woman came in with a beautiful alabaster jar of expensive perfume and poured it over his head. The disciples were indignant when they saw this. 'What a waste!' they said. 'It could have been sold for a high price and the money given to the poor.'**

    a)   Jesus sat in the homes of the most vulnerable people in society

Unlike many of us today, Jesus was able to go into the home of someone who in all likelihood would have been marginalised in society. If the truth be told, despite the vast number of medical advances in the last 2,000 years, most of us would struggle to sit and eat in the house of a leper today. Perhaps it is our inability to interact with the great and small in society which is limiting our influence. Christian leaders ought to ask themselves: how often do I interact with the despised and rejected in my society?

    b)   Jesus led his disciples to interact with the most vulnerable people in society

When Jesus went into Simon's house, it meant his disciples went to his house too. We know they were there because they reacted to what was going on in the house.

> Matthew 26:6 – Meanwhile, Jesus was in Bethany *at the home of Simon, a man who had previously had leprosy.*
>
> Matthew 26:8 – *The disciples were indignant* when they saw this. 'What a waste!' they said.

Sometimes, we cause our followers to do things that they would never have done had it not been because of our association with them.

9) *Pilate*

> Matthew 27:11 – Now Jesus was standing before Pilate, the Roman governor. 'Are you the king of the Jews?' the governor asked him. Jesus replied, 'You have said it.'

    a)   Jesus responded appropriately to secular authorities

When Jesus was brought before Pilate, he answered his questions respectfully. A good leader should respond appropriately to the secular authorities to which they are subject. Whether it be for tax purposes or the general law of the land, Christian leaders should abide by and comply with the law.

> Titus 3:1 – Remind the believers to submit to the government and its officers. They should be obedient, always ready to do what is good.

10) *Simon of Cyrene*

> Matthew 27:32 – Along the way, they came across a man named Simon, who was from Cyrene, and the soldiers forced him to carry Jesus' cross.

a) Jesus accepted the help of a complete stranger

After Jesus had been beaten, mocked and spat at, he was led away to be crucified. Having taken such a heavy beating, he must have been unable to carry his cross. The soldiers then recruited a stranger – Simon of Cyrene – to help Jesus. The lesson we can learn from this is that in our very weak moments, rather than our friends, family or loved ones coming to the rescue, we may in fact find help from strangers. This may come in the form of people we have never met or it may be a long-lost childhood friend who, after thirty years, is now a stranger to us. When this help is offered to us, we must honestly assess our circumstances and accept it.

In times of difficulty, it can be all too easy to lash out and reject suggestions and advice from people. However, we must be alert to the voice of the Holy Spirit so we can quickly identify when he is providing a supernatural lifeline from an unexpected and unknown source.

CHAPTER 6

JESUS' INTERACTIONS WITH THE PHARISEES

Throughout his ministry, Jesus faced opposition from the religious authorities. Whether it was intentional or well-meaning criticism we will never know, but the Gospel of Matthew tells us a story of a group of people who sought to keep Jesus in what they felt was his 'box'. This group, the Pharisees, thought Jesus lacked authority and should not have been doing the things he was doing.[10] They disagreed with virtually everything about him – his teachings and methods – and sought to reduce his influence on his followers. In this chapter, we will look at how Jesus responded to them when he interacted with the Pharisees and what lessons we can learn from these encounters.

---

10 In this chapter when referring to the Pharisees, I generally mean all religious leaders who opposed Jesus throughout his ministry, unless otherwise stated.

1) *Your critics will always seek to question your motives and good deeds*

> **Matthew 12:9–11** – Then Jesus went over to their synagogue, where he noticed a man with a deformed hand. The Pharisees asked Jesus, '*Does the law permit a person to work* by healing on the Sabbath?' (They were hoping he would say yes, so they could bring charges against him.) And he answered, 'If you had a sheep that fell into a well on the Sabbath, wouldn't you work to pull it out? Of course you would. And how much more valuable is a person than a sheep! Yes, *the law permits a person to do good* on the Sabbath.'

As leaders, we must accept some people will not believe we have good intentions or motives. Many will seek to catch us out in the hope that what we are doing will be brought to nothing. We must be able to discern when people are seeking to trick us and destroy what we are doing. This may come about through apparently innocent questions and enquiries. We need to be aware of our enemies.

The first step to overcoming this sort of attack is to ensure our motives are in fact clean and pure. Jesus was able to overcome this as he had no ulterior motive or hidden agenda. He simply wanted to help the man who needed healing. This meant the Pharisees were unable to take the action they had intended against him.

2) *Good intentions and helping others will not always be well received*

> **Matthew 12:9–14** – Then Jesus went over to their synagogue, where he noticed a man with a deformed hand. The Pharisees asked Jesus, 'Does the law permit a person to work by healing on the Sabbath?' (They were hoping he would say yes, *so they could bring charges against him*.) And he answered, 'If you had a sheep that fell into a

well on the Sabbath, wouldn't you work to pull it out? Of course, you would. And how much more valuable is a person than a sheep! Yes, the law permits a person to do good on the Sabbath.' Then he said to the man, 'Hold out your hand.' So, the man held out his hand, and it was restored, just like the other one! Then *the Pharisees called a meeting to plot how to kill Jesus.*

The Pharisees were upset with Jesus for wanting to help someone else. Ordinarily, we might expect them to want to rejoice with the man as he received his healing, being religious leaders familiar with the Hebrew Bible.[11] The Old Testament teaches that we ought to weep with those who are weeping and therefore, by extension, rejoice with those who are rejoicing.[12]

However, rather than celebrate with the man, the Pharisees sought to trick Jesus. One explanation for this could be they were unhappy Jesus had the ability to do something they couldn't. Perhaps they were jealous and were displeased and disgruntled that Jesus inadvertently and unavoidably showed them in a poor light.

We must be alert to the idea many of our critics are lashing out and hoping we fail because of their own insecurities. Many people feel threatened by others they think can do more than *they* can, or can even do better. This is something we should bear in mind when we suddenly

---

11 I am using the terms Hebrew Bible and Old Testament interchangeably. The main differences between the two collections are the ordering of the books and the number of books. The Hebrew Bible counts Samuel, Kings and Chronicles as one book each rather than two, Ezra and Nehemiah are one book, and the Twelve Minor Prophets form a single volume.
12 This is a theme in the Hebrew Bible which Paul later explicitly stated in Romans 12:15.

face unexpected opposition, especially when the natural and correct response would be to join in the celebration rather than to criticise.

3) *Be wary of people who may feel you have publicly embarrassed them*

> **Matthew 12:14 – Then the Pharisees called a meeting to plot how to kill Jesus.**

After this encounter, the Pharisees gathered together and planned to destroy Jesus. Perhaps this was because they felt he had humiliated them publicly. We must be cautious of people who hold on to perceived hurts and embarrassments. It may be better to address such hurts directly, rather than allow them to fester and develop into a bigger problem. This applies to both our followers and to us as leaders. We too may be holding on to and harbouring past hurts and offences which, if left unchecked, may serve as distractions preventing us from achieving our goals. After this encounter, the Pharisees were preoccupied with only one thing – destroying and eliminating Jesus.

4) *Some questions from your critics should be engaged with and answered fully*

> **Matthew 19:3-12 – Some Pharisees came to him to test him. They asked, 'Is it lawful for a man to divorce his wife for any and every reason?' 'Haven't you read,' he replied, 'that at the beginning the Creator "made them male and female," and said, "For this reason a man will leave his father and mother and be united to his wife, and the two will become one flesh"? So they are no longer two, but one flesh. Therefore what God has joined together, let no one separate.' 'Why then,' they asked, 'did Moses command that a man give his wife a certificate of divorce and send her away?' Jesus replied, 'Moses permitted you to divorce your wives because your hearts were hard. But it was not this way from the beginning. I tell you that anyone who divorces his wife, except for**

> sexual immorality, and marries another woman commits adultery.' The disciples said to him, 'If this is the situation between a husband and wife, it is better not to marry.' Jesus replied, 'Not everyone can accept this word, but only those to whom it has been given. For there are eunuchs who were born that way, and there are eunuchs who have been made eunuchs by others—and there are those who choose to live like eunuchs for the sake of the kingdom of heaven. The one who can accept this should accept it.' (NIV)

Again, the Pharisees came to Jesus with the aim of trapping him. But in this instance Jesus answered all their questions clearly and directly. He did not change the topic, tell a parable or ignore them. Instead, he debated with them and gave us a comprehensive teaching on marriage and divorce. His teaching on this topic was so engaging that even his disciples got involved in the discussion.

> Matthew 19:10 – Jesus' disciples then said to him, 'If this is the case, it is better not to marry!'

We must therefore be flexible when relating to our critics, as difficult as it may sound; Jesus' approach to his critics was not a one-size-fits-all strategy. It is critical we learn to discern what is the required response to our critics at any given time. Had Jesus not engaged the Pharisees and continued the discussion with his disciples, we would not have this crucial teaching on marriage.

5) *To be a vessel of change (disrupter) in an existing structure, you must have authority with both God and man*

> Matthew 21:12 – Jesus entered the Temple and began to drive out all the people buying and selling animals for sacrifice. He knocked over the tables of the money changers and the chairs of those selling doves.

We often have fantastical ideas about how we can change an existing structure or organisation, but the truth is we often lack the authority to make such changes. We are then frustrated and, in some instances, respond negatively to those in authority within these structures.

It is common practice for Christians to use this passage to incite people to be disrupters in culture and their churches, but one thing is often forgotten. This incident took place towards the end of Jesus' ministry; it occurs in the twenty-first chapter of a book with twenty-eight chapters. So we must keep in mind that, before Jesus went into the Temple to disrupt it, he already had a certain level of authority with both men and God. He already had a name worth following and the ability to set right what needed to be right in the Temple. The people went to him for healing and the children praised him, after he disrupted the Temple, because of the power endowed on him by God.

> Matthew 21:14–15 – The blind and the lame came to him in the Temple, and he healed them. The leading priests and the teachers of religious law saw these wonderful miracles and heard even the children in the Temple shouting, 'Praise God for the Son of David.'

The question then becomes how do we gain authority with God, which in turn leads to authority with men? There are two ways to gain authority with God in the Bible:

a) Study and know the Word of God

> 2 Timothy 2:15 – Study to shew thyself approved unto God, a workman that needeth not to be ashamed, rightly dividing the word of truth. (KJV)

To gain authority and approval by God we need to study and immerse ourselves in the Bible. We know Jesus did this, because he regularly quoted from the Hebrew Bible. It is easy to forget the Old Testament was not as accessible to people 2,000 years ago as it is to us now. Jesus did not have a Bible app, or a pocket printed Bible. He probably did not have a copy of the Hebrew Bible in his home. In all likelihood, the only access he had to the Old Testament would have been in the local synagogue or at his school. Yet he was able to memorise and quote verses from it freely. This must have taken hard work and many hours to learn. Again, we should be reminded that, although he is God, Jesus was a man and therefore had the very same experiences we have. If it is difficult for you or me to learn verses, it was difficult for him. But he did it.

> **Hebrews 4:15 – This High Priest [Jesus] of ours understands our weaknesses, for he faced all of the same testings we do, yet he did not sin.**

In this very passage, Jesus quotes directly from the Hebrew Bible twice.

> **Matthew 21:13 – He said to them, 'The Scriptures declare, "My Temple will be called a house of prayer," but you have turned it into a den of thieves!'**

> **Isaiah 56:7 – I will bring them to my holy mountain of Jerusalem and will fill them with joy in *my house of prayer*.**

> **Jeremiah 7:11 – Don't you yourselves admit that this Temple, which bears my name, has become a *den of thieves*? Surely, I see all the evil going on there. I, the Lord, have spoken!**

> **Matthew 21:16 – They asked Jesus, 'Do you hear what these children are saying?' 'Yes,' Jesus replied. 'Haven't you ever read the Scriptures? For they say, "You have taught children and infants to give you praise."'**

> **Psalm 8:2 – You have taught children and infants to tell of your strength [praise],**[13] **silencing your enemies and all who oppose you.**

It is worth noting the religious leaders were unable to dispute his words because he quoted directly from the Bible. As Christian leaders, we should determine to develop our ability to rightly divide the word of truth, which in turn leads to authority with God and men. If we are hoping to bring about major changes to the wider Church, we must have a solid foundation, rooted in the Word of God. Meaningful and lasting change will not come about if it is not grounded in the Scriptures.

Martin Luther gave birth to the Protestant movement because he read his Bible and saw the way Christianity was being practised did not reflect the teachings in the Bible.[14] Here, we see an example of a meaningful and long-standing change centred and rooted in the study of the Word of God. I don't think it is too far a stretch to claim I am writing this book today partly because of the radical change Martin Luther brought about. I believe revival will only come when we are focused on studying and understanding the Word of God.

  b) Long periods of prayer

Jesus spent long times in prayer. This is discussed extensively in the chapter on what Jesus did when he was alone. His prayer life was so exemplary that his disciples asked him to teach them how to pray.

---

13 Greek text (The Septuagint – LXX) reads praise.
14 Martin Luther, *The Ninety-Five Theses and Other Writings*, trans. William Russell (New York: Penguin Books, 2017).

> **Luke 11:1** – Once Jesus was in a certain place praying. As he finished, one of his disciples came to him and said, 'Lord, teach us to pray, just as John taught his disciples.'

Jacob wrestled with the Lord all night and received a new name and a blessing.

> **Genesis 32:24–30** – So Jacob was left alone, and a man wrestled with him till daybreak. When the man saw that he could not overpower him, he touched the socket of Jacob's hip so that his hip was wrenched as he wrestled with the man. Then the man said, 'Let me go, for it is daybreak.' But Jacob replied, 'I will not let you go unless you bless me.' The man asked him, 'What is your name?' 'Jacob,' he answered. Then the man said, *'Your name will no longer be Jacob, but Israel, because you have struggled with God and with humans and have overcome.'* Jacob said, 'Please tell me your name.' But he replied, 'Why do you ask my name?' Then he blessed him there. So Jacob called the place Peniel, saying, 'It is because I saw God face to face, and yet my life was spared.' (NIV)

To receive the authority we need to bring about the change God has placed in our hearts, we must be unrelenting in our pursuit for him through prayer. Jacob was determined not to leave the presence of God until he got what he needed. We must not give up seeking God until we see the answer to our prayers.

6) *Not everyone will be happy with what you are doing*

> **Matthew 21:15** – The leading priests and the teachers of religious law saw these wonderful miracles and heard even the children in the Temple shouting, 'Praise God for the Son of David.' But the leaders were indignant.

A leader should be aware that not everyone will like what they are doing. Your actions and very existence may stir up resentment and, in extreme cases, cause people to hate you. This does not mean you have to react. Jesus did not react to the indignation with malice or hatred; he only answered the question and provided an explanation for the actions of the people.

7) *Jesus knew when to walk away from a heated debate and go somewhere totally different to defuse the situation*

> **Matthew 21:15–17 – The leading priests and the teachers of religious law saw these wonderful miracles and heard even the children in the Temple shouting, 'Praise God for the Son of David.' But the leaders were *indignant*. They asked Jesus, 'Do you hear what these children are saying?' 'Yes,' Jesus replied. 'Haven't you ever read the Scriptures? For they say, "You have taught children and infants to give you praise."' Then he returned to Bethany, where he stayed overnight.**

Not every argument needs to be taken up, not every battle needs to be won. Seeing that the leaders were angry, Jesus responded and walked away. There was no further comment or response by the leaders. Perhaps this is because Jesus left before it escalated into something more aggressive. He actually left Jerusalem and went to a different town and stayed there overnight.

A good leader must learn the art of politely ending a conversation and moving on. Sometimes this will mean moving away entirely and leaving enough time for the issue to die down. Many debates and discussions not only increase tension and heighten differences and divisions, but are also a waste of time.

When I see that a disagreement is going on for more than five minutes, neither of us is changing our position and we are becoming more entrenched in our views, I often ask myself what is the aim of this discussion? If I can't quite pinpoint a valid reason for the discussion, I begin to round up and move on respectfully. Time is a valuable commodity that needs to be measured. Arguments are often not worth the time spent debating.

8) *Walking away from a place does not mean walking away forever*

> **Matthew 21:18 – In the morning, as Jesus was returning to Jerusalem, he was hungry,**

Jesus returned to Jerusalem the very next day. After a confrontation, issue or failure it is still possible to go back to the very place you have left. Walking away does not necessarily mean leaving a place or thing forever. Sometimes people walk away from a place or person indefinitely, when all that was needed was a break. It may be a short break of a few hours or a longer break of a few years, but it does not mean the door has been shut. People often prematurely bolt the door down permanently and miss opportunities or the fulfilment of their dream or vision. Had Jesus not returned to Jerusalem, there would not have been a last supper, there would have been no crucifixion or resurrection and, by extension, no Christianity.

9) *You do not have to answer every question thrown at you by your critics*

> **Matthew 21:23–27 – When Jesus returned to the Temple and began teaching, the leading priests and elders came up to him. They demanded, 'By what authority are you doing all these things? Who gave you the right?' 'I'll tell you by what authority I do these things if you answer one question,' Jesus replied. 'Did John's authority to baptize come from heaven, or was it merely human?' They talked it**

> over among themselves. 'If we say it was from heaven, he will ask us why we didn't believe John. But if we say it was merely human, we'll be mobbed because the people believe John was a prophet.' So, they finally replied, 'We don't know.' And Jesus responded, 'Then I won't tell you by what authority I do these things.'

Many times, people challenge and confront us using logic and reasons they do not apply to themselves or others. Jesus knew this when the Pharisees questioned his authority. For that reason, he asked them if they knew from where John the Baptist got his authority. Jesus' critics were unable to answer his question because they knew they would be made to look like fools. Rather than answer his question with what they thought might be true, they chose to lie to save face. This response reveals the motive behind their original question; it was not about putting things in order in the Temple or even correcting Jesus for breaking a law: it was all about making themselves look good in front of the people. The Pharisees could not stomach the fact Jesus was teaching with authority in the Temple and people were listening to him intently.

We need to be able to discern when we are being challenged simply because of jealousy and envy. Such challenges do not warrant a response, especially when it is clear the same criticism or reasoning is not being applied across the board.

10) A leader should be aware people can and will change their minds about their leadership

> Matthew 21:28–31 – 'But what do you think about this? A man with two sons told the older boy, "Son, go out and work in the vineyard today." The son answered, "No, I won't go," but later he changed his mind and went anyway. Then the father told the other son, "You go," and he said, "Yes, sir, I will." But he didn't go. Which of the two obeyed his father?"' They replied, 'The first.' Then Jesus explained his meaning:

> **'I tell you the truth, corrupt tax collectors and prostitutes will get into the Kingdom of God before you do.'**

People can and will change their minds about you at any time. Some people may say they are with you and will support you one hundred per cent but then change their minds about you without any warning. They may suddenly leave or begin to ignore you. Others may initially be unsure of you and be unwilling to commit themselves to your vision, but as time goes on, they may change their minds and become your biggest advocates. A leader must be willing to allow people to freely change their minds and be prepared for it.

11) *Rejection may come from those already doing what you want to do*

> **Matthew 21:42 – Then Jesus asked them, 'Didn't you ever read this in the Scriptures? "The stone that the builders rejected has now become the cornerstone. This is the Lord's doing, and it is wonderful to see."'**

Have you ever tried to reach out to someone for advice or support but been rejected? Perhaps you have been told you don't have the right qualities to do the job by someone who is already successful in that area? In this verse, Jesus teaches us a powerful lesson: the stone the builders, namely the people working with knowledge and experience, have rejected is the very one that will become the cornerstone – the main stone all the other stones in the building will depend upon.

We should not be disheartened if those in a position of authority disregard or reject our vision. We should hold on to our dream and watch and wait for God to lift us up. It will become clear and evident to all, in the fullness of time, that it is the Lord's doing and it is indeed marvellous in our sight!

12) *The enemy is in the business of plotting and setting traps for you to fall*

> **Matthew 22:15–18 –** *Then the Pharisees went and plotted how they might entangle Him in His talk.* **And they sent to Him their disciples with the Herodians, saying, 'Teacher, we know that You are true, and teach the way of God in truth; nor do You care about anyone, for You do not regard the person of men. Tell us, therefore, what do You think? Is it lawful to pay taxes to Caesar, or not?' But Jesus perceived their wickedness, and said, 'Why do you test Me, you hypocrites?'** (NKJV)

As Christians, we must always remember there is an enemy whose sole aim is to bring to nothing all we are trying to build. It often feels as though we are fighting various battles on different fronts; at work, home and church. We must remember our battle is not against flesh-and-blood enemies, but against a spiritual, unseen enemy.

> **Ephesians 6:12 – For we are not fighting against flesh-and-blood enemies, but against evil rulers and authorities of the unseen world, against mighty powers in this dark world, and against evil spirits in the heavenly places.**

The ultimate aim of our unseen enemy is to destroy us.

> **John 10:10 – The thief's purpose is to steal and kill and destroy.**

With this in mind, we should not be shocked the enemy is constantly plotting on how to bring about our downfall. Here, the Pharisees were just a vehicle used by the enemy to bring about Jesus' demise. This was not the first time they tried to trick Jesus, and it was not the last time in the Gospel of Matthew. We should, therefore, be ready to respond to the enemy's traps. As Paul taught the Corinthians, we should not be ignorant to the schemes of the enemy; but know there is someone out there whose main aim is to prevent us from becoming all that God has called us to be.

> **2 Corinthians 2:11 – Lest Satan should get an advantage of (outsmart) us: for we are not ignorant of his devices. (KJV)**

13) Honesty and sincerity will disarm your enemies

> **Matthew 22:15–22 – Then the Pharisees went and plotted how they might entangle Him in His talk. And they sent to Him their disciples with the Herodians, saying, 'Teacher, we know that You are true, and teach the way of God in truth; nor do You care about anyone, for You do not regard the person of men. Tell us, therefore, what do You think? Is it lawful to pay taxes to Caesar, or not?' But Jesus perceived their wickedness, and said, 'Why do you test Me, you hypocrites? Show Me the tax money.' So they brought Him a denarius. And He said to them, 'Whose image and inscription is this?' They said to Him, 'Caesar's.' And He said to them, 'Render therefore to Caesar the things that are Caesar's, and to God the things that are God's.' When they had heard these words, they marvelled, and left Him and went their way. (NKJV)**

Seemingly tough questions only have one response – the truth. Jesus did not fall for the plot against him by simply telling the truth. The truth was the law of the land dictated that taxes ought to be paid to Caesar, regardless of any political or religious differences at the time – that was the law that needed to be observed, and that is what Jesus told them. His enemies were not able to snare him by his words, because his words were based on a principle rather than on his emotions or feelings. Jesus may have thought the Roman government was illegitimate (unlikely), but that did not alter his approach to the law on taxation.

It was probably the case that the Pharisees sent their disciples to question Jesus, rather than go themselves, in the hope he would not recognise them and would therefore speak more freely against Caesar. However, Jesus was genuine and spoke as he would have spoken to anyone, in all sincerity and honesty. His truthful speech not only shocked those who came to trick him, but caused them to leave him alone. If we are consistent and honest in our speech, it will be difficult for our enemies to use our words against us. The truth has a way of startling those who seek to deceive and trap you.

14) A leader must abide by the laws and regulations of the land

> **Matthew 22:19–21 – 'Show Me the tax money.' So they brought Him a denarius. And He said to them, 'Whose image and inscription is this?' They said to Him, 'Caesar's.' And He said to them, *'Render therefore to Caesar the things that are Caesar's, and to God the things that are God's.'* When they had heard these words, they marvelled, and left Him and went their way. (NKJV)**

It goes without saying, but a good leader must abide by all the laws of the territory they find themselves in or hope to operate in. Breaking the rules often leads to dishonesty and puts you in a place of vulnerability where people can have an unnecessary hold over you.

15) To survive, a leader needs stamina, determination, consistency and strength

> **Matthew 22:23–46 –** *The same day the Sadducees, who say there is no resurrection,* **came to Him and asked Him, saying: 'Teacher, Moses said that if a man dies, having no children, his brother shall marry his wife and raise up offspring for his brother. Now there were with us seven brothers. The first died after he had married, and having no offspring, left his wife to his brother. Likewise the second also, and the third, even to the seventh. Last of all the woman died also. Therefore, in the resurrection, whose wife of the seven will she be? For they all had her.' Jesus answered and said to them, 'You are mistaken, not knowing the**

> Scriptures nor the power of God. For in the resurrection they neither marry nor are given in marriage, but are like angels of God in heaven.
>
> 'But concerning the resurrection of the dead, *have you not read what was spoken to you by God*, saying, "I am the God of Abraham, the God of Isaac, and the God of Jacob"? God is not the God of the dead, but of the living.' And when the multitudes heard this, they were astonished at His teaching. But when the Pharisees heard that He had silenced the Sadducees, they gathered together. Then one of them, a lawyer, asked Him a question, testing Him, and saying, 'Teacher, which is the great commandment in the law?' Jesus said to him, '"You shall love the Lord your God with all your heart, with all your soul, and with all your mind." This is the first and great commandment. And the second is like it: "You shall love your neighbor as yourself." On these two commandments hang all the Law and the Prophets.'
>
> While the Pharisees were gathered together, Jesus asked them, saying, 'What do you think about the Christ? Whose Son is He?' They said to Him, 'The Son of David.' He said to them, 'How then does David in the Spirit call Him "Lord," saying: "The Lord said to my Lord, 'Sit at My right hand, Till I make Your enemies Your footstool'"? If David then calls Him "Lord," how is He his Son?' And no one was able to answer Him a word, nor from that day on did anyone dare question Him anymore. (NKJV)

a) Consistency

Immediately after Jesus had overcome the trap set by the Pharisees, a second group of people approached him with another trap. The Sadducees did not believe in the resurrection, yet they asked him a question based on something they did not support or believe in.

True to form, Jesus responded to this trick question with a tried and tested method: he quoted the Scriptures.

Not only had this method worked with the Pharisees, but this was the same method he used to defeat the devil in the wilderness and was the same method used in the succeeding verses.[15] In some instances one does not need to change tactics to defeat an enemy; one just needs to remain consistent. Sometimes the enemy comes again with the same test to see if our survival the first time was a fluke, a one-off response. Perhaps we just got lucky? We therefore need to remain consistent to overcome the enemy.

b) Stamina, determination and strength

In this chapter alone, Jesus was interrogated by the religious leaders no fewer than three times. It got to a point where the Pharisees used their most skilled legal expert to question Jesus, in the hope he would be defeated.

> **Matthew 22:15–16 – Then the Pharisees went and plotted together how they might trap Him in what He said. And they sent their disciples to Him, along with the Herodians, saying, 'Teacher, we know that You are truthful and teach the way of God in truth, and defer to no one; for You are not partial to any.' (NASB)**

> **Matthew 22:23 – On that day some Sadducees (who say there is no resurrection) came to Jesus and questioned Him,** [about the brothers marrying the widow]. **(NASB)**

> **Matthew 22:34–35 – But when the Pharisees heard that Jesus had silenced the Sadducees, they gathered themselves together. One of them, a lawyer, asked Him a question, testing Him,** [about the most important commandment]. **(NASB)**

---

15 See chapter 7 – 'What did Jesus do when he was alone?' for a discussion on the devil and the wilderness.

For Jesus to have survived this level of intense scrutiny and questioning, he must have developed stamina. Many times, we give up at the first sign of opposition, or sometimes the second, but the key is to fight on until your enemy is tired. That is exactly what Jesus did.

> **Matthew 22:46 – No one was able to answer Him a word, nor did anyone dare from that day on to ask Him another question. (NASB)**

We must be determined to outplay our enemies and remain strong in the process. At one stage in the debate with the lawyer, Jesus turned the tables and started questioning him. Jesus was not intimated by the number of people around him, or by who was questioning him or what they were saying.

> **Matthew 22:41–42 – Then, surrounded by the Pharisees, Jesus asked them a question: 'What do you think about the Messiah? Whose son is he?'**

The enemy does not give up easily and will try to come back stronger to defeat us. We must be ready for this by developing strength, stamina and determination. Like Jesus, we must be prepared to go toe-to-toe with our enemies until all their questions are answered and resolved.

16) Knowledge and preparation will always set leaders above their followers and critics

As previously mentioned, the Sadducees asked Jesus a question based on a doctrine they did not believe in. Sometimes we are tested so that our logic, motives and ways of thinking are exposed. Often, we are thrown off balance because there are gaps in our logic. Perhaps we lack knowledge in a certain area or we have not done enough preparation for the task we are confronting.

Jesus was able to respond to the questioning because he knew more than the Sadducees. He understood and knew their doctrine. He could explain to them why they were wrong, based on doctrine and principles they both agreed and accepted to be true.

We often go into a task unprepared or lacking knowledge and expect God just to show up. This is of course possible, but if we have knowledge and are well read across a number of fields, it is more likely we will win the respect of our critics, even if they don't agree with us. Jesus was able to get to the heart of the Sadducees' problem, that they did not understand the resurrection and God's power, because he knew more about them and the Scriptures than they did about him.

As a theology student, one of the things we are taught when it comes to discussions on science and religion is that many scientists don't know much about Christianity and many Christians don't know very much about science. Frequently in debates, there is conflict because each side may be talking over the other side, not fully understanding the concepts or language of each field. Very often in discussions, either side may be mocked or ridiculed, which in turn makes the opposing side switch off. Perhaps, if more Christians (outside academia) fully understood the complex theories in science, a more meaningful discussion could be had and more scientists would embrace Christianity?

17) A leader must be blameless

> **Matthew 26:59–60 – Inside, the leading priests and the entire high council were trying to find witnesses who would lie about Jesus, so they could put him to death. But even though they found many who agreed to give false witness, they could not use anyone's testimony.**

One of the things that sets Jesus apart from all of us is that he was blameless. The council sought for something to hold against him but found nothing. It was so difficult that even when people tried to lie about him, their accounts did not add up, which made it difficult to use their testimony. As leaders, we must aim to be blameless on all fronts, especially if we are looking to be leaders in the Church.

> **1 Timothy 3:1–2 – This is a trustworthy saying: 'If someone aspires to be a church leader, he desires an honorable position.' So a church leader must be a man whose life is above reproach [blameless].**

If we are blameless in as many areas as possible, it will be difficult for people to sling mud at us and for that mud to stick.

18) *Silence is sometimes the best remedy*

> **Matthew 27:12–14 – But when the leading priests and the elders made their accusations against him, Jesus remained silent. 'Don't you hear all these charges they are bringing against you?' Pilate demanded. But Jesus made no response to any of the charges, much to the governor's surprise.**

Jesus was accused by the chief priests and elders but remained silent. His silence was so deafening that Pilate was shocked and basically told Jesus to defend himself, yet he still remained silent. Not only was Jesus silent at his trial, but he was silent throughout his torture and crucifixion.

> **Matthew 27:15–45 – Now at the feast the governor was accustomed to releasing to the multitude one prisoner whom they wished. And at that time they had a notorious prisoner called Barabbas. Therefore, when they had gathered together, Pilate said to them, 'Whom do you want me to release to you? Barabbas, or Jesus who is called Christ?' For he knew that they had handed Him over because of envy. While he was sitting on the judgment seat, his wife sent to him, saying, 'Have**

nothing to do with that just Man, for I have suffered many things today in a dream because of Him.'

But the chief priests and elders persuaded the multitudes that they should ask for Barabbas and destroy Jesus. The governor answered and said to them, 'Which of the two do you want me to release to you?' They said, 'Barabbas!' Pilate said to them, 'What then shall I do with Jesus who is called Christ?' They all said to him, 'Let Him be crucified!' Then the governor said, 'Why, what evil has He done?' But they cried out all the more, saying, 'Let Him be crucified!' When Pilate saw that he could not prevail at all, but rather that a tumult was rising, he took water and washed his hands before the multitude, saying, 'I am innocent of the blood of this just Person. You see to it.' And all the people answered and said, 'His blood be on us and on our children.' Then he released Barabbas to them; and when he had scourged Jesus, he delivered Him to be crucified.

Then the soldiers of the governor took Jesus into the Praetorium and gathered the whole garrison around Him. And they stripped Him and put a scarlet robe on Him. When they had twisted a crown of thorns, they put it on His head, and a reed in His right hand. And they bowed the knee before Him and mocked Him, saying, '"Hail, King of the Jews!' Then they spat on Him, and took the reed and struck Him on the head. And when they had mocked Him, they took the robe off Him, put His own clothes on Him, and led Him away to be crucified.

Now as they came out, they found a man of Cyrene, Simon by name. Him they compelled to bear His cross. And when they had come to a place called Golgotha, that is to say, Place of a Skull, they gave Him sour wine mingled with gall to drink. But when He had tasted it, He would not drink. Then they crucified Him, and divided His garments, casting lots, that it might be fulfilled which was spoken by the prophet: 'They divided My garments among them, And for My clothing they cast lots.' Sitting down, they kept watch over Him there. And they put up

> over His head the accusation written against Him: **THIS IS JESUS THE KING OF THE JEWS.** Then two robbers were crucified with Him, one on the right and another on the left.
>
> And those who passed by blasphemed Him, wagging their heads and saying, 'You who destroy the temple and build it in three days, save Yourself! If You are the Son of God, come down from the cross.' Likewise the chief priests also, mocking with the scribes and elders, said, 'He saved others; Himself He cannot save. If He is the King of Israel, let Him now come down from the cross, and we will believe Him. He trusted in God; let Him deliver Him now if He will have Him; for He said, "I am the Son of God."' Even the robbers who were crucified with Him reviled Him with the same thing.
>
> Now from the sixth hour until the ninth hour there was darkness over all the land. (NKJV)

It gets to a point where silence is the only remedy and response to critics. Jesus' silence throughout his trial and crucifixion is perhaps one of the most striking features of his story. It is taught widely and admired by Christians and non-Christians. It has influenced charities and is a foundation for ideas such as Christian pacifism.[16] Many civil rights activists in 1960s America were influenced by Jesus' response and gained widespread support because of it.[17]

---

16 Christian Aid seeks aid in the development of 'peaceful and effective alternatives to violence and armed conflict' – 'From Violence to Peace: What we do', Christian Aid, www.christianaid.org.uk/about-us/what-we-do/tackling-violence-building-peace.

17 Perhaps the most noteworthy example of this was Martin Luther King Jr, who won the Nobel Peace Prize in 1964 for using non-violent resistance to racial oppression. In his Justice Without Violence speech, King makes reference to Jesus' remark to Peter to 'put up' his sword. King's point being that the bloodshed of many throughout history would have been prevented had

Silence should never be viewed as a sign of weakness, as it often acts as a positive testimony against one's accusers. Jesus was able to hold his tongue without feeling the need to defend himself or correct the false judgements and conclusions made about him. He did not feel that he needed to fix the injustice he was experiencing. We need to ask ourselves constantly how long we can remain silent without feeling the need to defend ourselves or express our unhappiness at an injustice we are experiencing.

On the day I read this passage for my quiet time, I found myself in a local supermarket. I was in the queue for the till waiting to be served. To observe social distancing, one of the shop assistants moved the queue so we ended up queuing down an empty aisle. As I was moving, another customer joined the queue ahead of me and jumped the line. I was upset and looked to the shop assistant, hoping she would tell the lady she had jumped in. But she didn't, and told me to move back to maintain the two-metre distance rule. I was annoyed and remember saying to myself, 'This isn't fair; she jumped the queue.'

I then recalled this passage and thought to myself, 'This really isn't that important – and even if it was, Christ did not respond when he experienced injustice, why is this such a big deal?' In our daily routines and activities, we must let go of knee-jerk reactions to fight, and instead manage to let go of such small personal injustices.

---

       this advice been heeded. – 'King Quotes on War and Peace,' King Institute Stanford University, https://kinginstitute.stanford.edu/liberation-curriculum/classroom-resources/king-quotes-war-and-peace.

CHAPTER 7

WHAT DID JESUS DO WHEN HE WAS ALONE?

So far, we have examined the leadership qualities Jesus exemplified in his encounters and interactions with different groups of people. But perhaps the most critical leadership qualities we can learn from are the ones he developed in secret, when he was alone. As Christians, we tend not to discuss or make reference to the moments in the Scriptures when Jesus is described as being alone. I think this often means we respond incorrectly to our own 'alone' moments. We assume we have been abandoned by God or have misheard from God about our vision, calling or gifts.

I believe that by examining and understanding what Jesus did when he was alone, it will not only highlight that he was more like us than we can imagine, but also encourage us to develop key qualities that will make us better leaders and inspire the people we lead.

> **Matthew 4:1-2** – Then was Jesus led up of the Spirit into the wilderness to be tempted of the devil. And when he had fasted forty days and forty nights, he was afterward an hungred. (KJV)

1) Be led by the Holy Spirit into the wilderness

Matthew 4:1 – Then was Jesus led up of the Spirit into the wilderness.

It sounds counterintuitive, but to fulfil our callings we have to learn how to follow the Holy Spirit into the wilderness or, more bluntly, into a ditch. A wilderness by definition is an uncultivated, uninhabited and inhospitable region. It is a place of deep loneliness and solitude. Many of us have experienced wilderness moments in our lives but have rejected them (often in Jesus' name). Rather than seek for God, we have turned to friends, crowds or turned back to our old, bad habits, and often lost sight of the vision God originally placed in our hearts. But this is not the aim of the wilderness.

It is in the wilderness that we are supposed to develop our relationship with the Father. I say develop because, to go to the wilderness, one must already be alert and alive to the voice of God. It is quite possible God has already placed a vision in your heart which you ought to fulfil but which has led you into the wilderness to focus on him.

I believe the Holy Spirit leads us into the wilderness to drown out the various voices which distract us and prevent us from fulfilling the will of God.[18] We should not be surprised if in the wilderness we lose friends, positions, relationships, money, careers or fall ill. This is because the wilderness is a place of neglect and abandonment.

The aim of the wilderness is to enhance our dependency on God. It is in the wilderness we are expected to seek the Father in a deeper way than we have before. We see it was in the wilderness that Jesus prayed

---

18 For further insight on hearing the voice of the Holy Spirit, see Dag Heward-Mills, *The Art of Hearing, 2nd Edition* (London: Parchment House, 2017).

and fasted for forty days. There is no other record of him fasting other than during this period.

In the wilderness we are supposed to learn how to hold fast to God even when we cannot hear him or get no response from him. It is in the wilderness that we are supposed to learn the art of overcoming the devil through the Word of God. Without any sort of supernatural encounter, we are meant to learn how to be utterly and totally dependent on the Bible as the source of our faith and strength. Notice that the angels ministered to Jesus after he overcame the devil with the Word of God. I believe we are led into the wilderness to build this crucial foundation.

It is imperative that, as God lifts us up, we are grounded and rooted in his word, so we are not ourselves tossed away by every wind of doctrine (Ephesians 4:14) or do not become castaways (1 Corinthians 9:27). As Paul instructed Timothy, we are supposed to pay close attention to the Word, so that we save both ourselves and those we will lead.

> **1 Timothy 4:16 – Take heed unto thyself, and *unto the doctrine*; continue in them: for in doing this *thou shalt both save thyself, and them that hear thee.* (KJV)**

2) *Seek the Father through prayer and fasting for long periods of time*

> **Matthew 4:2 – And when he had fasted forty days and forty nights, he was afterward an hungred. (KJV)**

Our alone times often occur before the fulfilment of the dream or vision about which we are seeking God, or else they are moments when the dream or vision looks as if it is impossible or far-fetched. In these moments, we should not wallow in self-pity, ignore the voice of God or follow the crowd. Instead, we should use this time to seek God and set the standard for our project or ministry. It is an opportunity to build ourselves up.

Jesus' baptism and the affirmation of the Father from heaven, although legitimising his ministry to the crowd who witnessed it, in all likelihood also reassured him that he was walking in God's will. We can liken this moment to our own moments where the Holy Spirit affirms our callings, gifts or projects.

The Bible teaches us Christ experienced all we have experienced.

> **Hebrews 4:14–15 – So then, since we have a great High Priest who has entered heaven, Jesus the Son of God … This High Priest of ours understands our weaknesses, *for he faced all of the same testings we do*, yet he did not sin.**

We often assume that because he was God, he was certain of his call. But while he was God, he was a man as well. We know he was tempted in all things, meaning in the same way we are often unsure about the call, ministry or project God has placed in our hearts, we should remember he too felt this insecurity.

It was after this confirmation that he went to pray and fast for forty days. We should also seek the Father through prayer and fasting when he confirms a vision to us.

3) *Overcome the devil.*

> **Matthew 4:3–11 – And when the tempter came to him, he said, 'If thou be the Son of God, command that these stones be made bread.' But he answered and said, 'It is written, "Man shall not live by bread alone, but by every word that proceedeth out of the mouth of God."' Then the devil taketh him up into the holy city, and setteth him on a**

pinnacle of the temple, and saith unto him, 'If thou be the Son of God, cast thyself down: for it is written, "He shall give his angels charge concerning thee: and in their hands they shall bear thee up, lest at any time thou dash thy foot against a stone."' Jesus said unto him, 'It is written again, "Thou shalt not tempt the Lord thy God."' Again, the devil taketh him up into an exceeding high mountain, and sheweth him all the kingdoms of the world, and the glory of them; And saith unto him, 'All these things will I give thee, if thou wilt fall down and worship me.' Then saith Jesus unto him, 'Get thee hence, Satan: for it is written, "Thou shalt worship the Lord thy God, and him only shalt thou serve."' Then the devil leaveth him, and, behold, angels came and ministered unto him. (KJV)

a) Overcome the devil with the Word of God

While in the wilderness, Jesus was able to overcome the devil alone. He did this using the Word of God. We frequently try to overcome the devil using our minds or by calling a friend, but our greatest weapon against the enemy is the Word of God. How do we know this? This is the method Jesus used to overcome him. Notice he had been in prayer for forty days but did not respond to the devil with prayer. He opened his mouth and quoted verses.

Jesus quoted directly from the book of Deuteronomy, three times:

> Deuteronomy 8:3 – So He humbled you, allowed you to hunger, and fed you with manna which you did not know nor did your fathers know, *that He might make you know that man shall not live by bread alone; but man lives by every word that proceeds from the mouth of the Lord.* (NKJV)

> Deuteronomy 6:16 – *Ye shall not tempt the Lord your God*, as ye tempted him in Massah. (KJV)

> **Deuteronomy 6:13** – *Thou shalt fear the Lord thy God, and serve him, and shalt swear by his name.* (KJV)

It is worth noting the devil quoted from the Word of God too, in the second temptation.

> **Psalm 91:11** – For He shall give His angels charge over you, to keep you in all your ways. (NKJV)

This tells us the devil is well aware of the power of the Word of God. It also tells us that just because the Bible is being used to cause us to act in a way contrary to what we know to be true, it does not necessarily mean it is correct. Our response to such contradictions should still be the Word of God. How then do we know when we are entering into unnecessary arguments or rejecting a legitimate correction?

When the devil tempted Christ with the second temptation, Jesus responded with another verse. The devil did not reply with yet another verse to support his initial argument. He did not even try to use a verse for the third temptation. It was as though he was using the Bible to throw dust into Jesus' eyes, as a distraction. It was as though he was using it to manipulate Jesus into doing what he wanted rather than to aid or genuinely correct him. I think this is how we can know when the Bible is being used incorrectly. Additionally, we have the witness of the Holy Spirit. I have found that if I am corrected by the Word of God but I am initially reluctant to accept what is being said, after the event the Holy Spirit reminds me of what was said and points me to another verse to support what has been shared.

> **John 14:26** – But the Helper, *the Holy Spirit*, whom the Father will send in My name, He will teach you all things, *and bring to your remembrance all things that I said to you.* (NKJV)

Jesus was able to overcome the devil by holding fast to the Word of God. The Gospel of Luke teaches us that, from a young age, Jesus was in the Temple reasoning with the scribes concerning the Scriptures.

> **Luke 2:46–47 – And it came to pass, that after three days they found him in the temple, sitting in the midst of the doctors, both hearing them, and asking them questions. And all that heard him were astonished at his understanding and answers. (KJV)**

This reveals that we are supposed to spend a portion of our time learning and acquainting ourselves with the Bible. It is our responsibility to interrogate and understand the Word of God to the best of our ability, so that when the enemy comes to attack us, we are fully equipped. The Word of God is our greatest weapon against the enemy.

> **Ephesians 4:17 – And take the helmet of salvation, and the sword of the Spirit, which is the word of God. (KJV)**

When we look at the wider ministry of Jesus, it is clear this ability to overcome the enemy was an essential component. Throughout his ministry, Jesus was able to answer his critics and opponents. I believe it was easy for him to outwit the Pharisees, Sadducees and others, including his disciples, because he had dealt with the devil alone in the wilderness.

Many of us struggle to overcome our enemies and opposition because we have not learnt to overcome the devil alone through the power of the Word of God. Rather than turning to the Bible, we turn to the phone, social media, TV or we look for a supernatural sign. We depend on someone else or something other than the Word of God. I believe if we are able to develop the art of depending on the Word of God as our sword in our battles, we will be one step closer to the fulfilment of the dream that God has placed in our hearts.

b) Overcome the devil by rebuking him

> **Matthew 4:8- Again, the devil taketh him up into an exceeding high mountain, and sheweth him all the kingdoms of the world, and the glory of them; And saith unto him, 'All these things will I give thee, if thou wilt fall down and worship me.'** *Then saith Jesus unto him, 'Get thee hence, Satan***: for it is written, "Thou shalt worship the Lord thy God, and him only shalt thou serve."'** *Then the devil leaveth* **him. (KJV)**

To overcome the final temptation, Jesus spoke directly to the devil and told him to leave – and he left. This was the first time Jesus rebuked Satan, but it was not the last. I believe that because he developed this habit when he was alone, he was able to identify Satan when he saw him in public.

> **Matthew 16:23 – But he [Jesus] turned, and said unto Peter, 'Get thee behind me, Satan: thou art an offence unto me: for thou savourest not the things that be of God, but those that be of men.' (KJV)**

4) *Preach*

> **Matthew 4:17–18 – From that time** *Jesus began to preach***, and to say, 'Repent: for the kingdom of heaven is at hand'. And Jesus, walking by the sea of Galilee, saw two brethren, Simon called Peter, and Andrew his brother, casting a net into the sea: for they were fishers. (KJV)**

After Jesus left the desert, he departed from Galilee. The Bible teaches us that he began to preach. At this time, he had no followers or disciples. He was alone, preaching his message of repentance. It was as he was walking that he saw and recruited his first disciples. What can we learn from this? Just start! Do what you feel the calling or conviction to do!

Jesus did not wait to have disciples, a following or a crowd before he started preaching. He started alone. It was his preaching which then converted his disciples. As leaders, we need to be willing and ready to start alone. We need to believe in and hold on to the calling and grace of God in our lives. Just because I am doing something alone, it doesn't mean it is wrong. Pioneers often start out alone, with no one to encourage them but the Holy Spirit.

It is this assurance and confidence which perhaps attracted Peter and John to his call and caused them to drop what they were doing to follow him. God will direct the right people into our lives who will drop what they are doing and follow us to fulfil the call or the vision God has placed in our hearts. All one needs to do is start, and the right people will show up at the right time.

5) *Jesus remained focused and was not distracted by the people around him*

> **Matthew 26:36–44** – Then cometh Jesus with them unto a place called Gethsemane, and saith unto the disciples, 'Sit ye here, while I go and pray yonder.' And he took with him Peter and the two sons of Zebedee, and began to be sorrowful and very heavy. Then saith he unto them, 'My soul is exceeding sorrowful, even unto death: tarry ye here, and watch with me.' And he went a little further, and fell on his face, and prayed, saying, 'O my Father, if it be possible, let this cup pass from me: nevertheless, not as I will, but as thou wilt.' And he cometh unto the disciples, and findeth them asleep, and saith unto Peter, 'What, could ye not watch with me one hour? Watch and pray, that ye enter not into temptation: the spirit indeed is willing, but the flesh is weak.' He went away again the second time, and prayed, saying, 'O my Father, if this cup may not pass away from me, except I drink it, thy will be done.' And he came and found them asleep again: for their eyes were heavy. And he left them, and went away again, and prayed the third time, saying the same words. (KJV)

As leaders, we are often distracted and discouraged by the people we are leading. In the Garden of Gethsemane, Jesus was in, quite possibly, his most vulnerable state. The Gospel tells us he was sorrowful and very heavy. He confided in his disciples about his anguish before withdrawing alone to pray to God. In this state, we would expect the disciples as his friends and confidants either to comfort him or to pray for or with him. But instead they fell asleep, not once, but twice. Despite this, Jesus remained focused on his prayer. He did not change his prayer topic and was not affected in any way by the disciples' inability to stay awake.

For many of us, this would have turned into an opportunity to complain to God about the type of people we have around us, or an opportunity to dress down our followers. Jesus, however, addressed the issue and quickly moved on from the weakness of the disciples and went back to what he was doing. Sometimes, we spend far too much time addressing the problems of the people with whom we are working and lose sight of the task ahead of us, the goal we are trying to achieve. This is often a distraction which probably achieves little more than alienating those with whom we are working, and it also wastes precious time. As leaders, it is essential we remain focused on what we are called to complete rather than on the inadequacies of the people around us.

6) Desertion

> **Matthew 26:56 – But all this was done, that the scriptures of the prophets might be fulfilled. Then all the disciples forsook him, and fled. (KJV)**

Jesus was abandoned and deserted by all his friends. I have found this is a point we often forget. It seems this is something we know about but we never totally embrace it and understand it. For me, one of the most difficult aspects of Christianity is understanding and accepting the call to be like Christ and to experience all he experienced on the road to the cross. The first main signpost on the road to the cross is abandonment and desertion. If we are able to embrace and accept this, it will be far easier to overcome when we experience it. We should remember there comes a time when every leader is deserted. If it happened to Jesus, it will happen to me. Recall that a servant is not above his master.

What does it mean to be abandoned and deserted on the road to the cross? It means to expect and accept loneliness. It means to be hurt by those who are most dear to us. It means to be disappointed by those we least expect to disappoint us. It means to be left alone by those we have confided in and depended upon. This is likely to occur at our weakest and lowest moments, or when we least expect it.

Remember, a few verses before, Jesus told the disciples he was sorrowful and heavy. His disciples knew something bad was about to happen and Jesus was anxious about it, yet they still fled. The thought of standing with their teacher, mentor, pastor and friend did not enter their minds. They smelt danger and knew they had to protect themselves. That was it. It was not personal – it was an act driven by the natural human instinct to survive.

It is worth understanding the rationale behind the disciples' actions, so we can imagine it as it was rather than as part of a 2,000-year-old story, which can often seem abstract and unreal. When we understand it in this way, we can relate better not only to the disciples but also to Jesus Christ as he was arrested that night in the garden. We are now able to see that, like so many of us, despite being God, at his most vulnerable Jesus encountered something similar to what so many of us have also experienced. He was abandoned by his very best friends at the time he needed them most. He had done what was correct and proper – took his concerns and fears to God – and was still alone, rejected and deserted. This should remind us, when we not only *feel* alone but are actually alone that, just like Jesus, we are on the road to glory but must endure our season of desertion before we arrive at our final destination.

We should not feel the need to pay back those who have abandoned us or embrace the people we have left behind in the world to fill the void left by those who have forsaken us. Our response should not be shock or disappointment in God. Instead, we ought to embrace what God has called us to and hold on to the promise of glory, just as Christ has taught us to do.

CONCLUSION

By examining the interactions between Jesus and the cast of Matthew's Gospel through the lens of his humanity, we have gained insight into his unique leadership style.

In accepting and embracing the humanity of Jesus, we have seen that we as leaders have probably experienced and suffered many of the same things as him in our interactions with the people we are called to lead.

From Jesus' interactions with God the Father, we learnt it is totally acceptable at one stage or another to feel abandoned by God the Father. We also saw that Jesus was a man of his word. He practised what he taught the disciples about prayer; he prayed secretly in private and was openly rewarded.

His interactions with the disciples taught us a number of things; too many to summarise in this conclusion, but what is clear is that we will not always be understood by the people we are leading. This does not mean these people should be easily thrown away; rather, if we are committed to correcting and encouraging them, these are the people who will support us and take our vision and dream to new heights.

The relationship between Jesus and Judas is interesting and speaks to perhaps one of the greatest leadership qualities of Jesus Christ. In this relationship, we see Jesus was forgiving and did not hold the mistakes of his followers against them.

The minor characters of the Gospel reveal that Jesus was concerned with the random people he encountered in his day-to-day dealings. In every random encounter, a life was changed and encouraged. These spontaneous encounters led to an increased following and gave Jesus greater influence in the towns he visited. We are therefore reminded as leaders not to despise the seemingly insignificant interactions we have with people who may not at first glance appear to shape or change our world.

When interacting with the Pharisees, we learnt that Jesus did not always respond the same way. Every situation called for a different response; there was no uniform approach to his interactions with his critics. Perhaps the one certain thing was that Jesus knew more than those criticising him. He was never caught off guard by their attacks. We learnt that a leader should be well prepared and ready to respond where the circumstances require it.

In withdrawing from the crowds and spending time alone, Jesus developed a number of key qualities I think contributed to his leadership skills. It is crucial that, like Jesus, leaders separate themselves from the crowd. Separation and withdrawal enable us to develop foundational qualities we can hold on to for the future as our vision and dreams unfold. Jesus developed the art of praying. In his alone times, he maintained his aim and did what he was called to do way before anyone else believed in him. These are the skills leaders must develop if they hope to gain a large and lasting following like Jesus Christ – the Greatest Leader of All Time.

EPILOGUE

If you aren't a Christian and you made it to the end of this book, thank you for bearing with me. Not everything contained in this book will apply to you or seem relevant. However, as you will have found, leaving aside the more 'spiritual' or miraculous accounts in the Gospel of Matthew, there is practical and useful wisdom that can be gleaned from the life and words of Jesus Christ. I hope you are able to apply this knowledge to your organisation, life or business, for the better.

If this book has made you more curious about Christianity and the life of Jesus Christ, then why not take a peek at the other Gospels – Mark, Luke and John? I guarantee you there are wisdom and knowledge to be found in them too. I would also suggest, where possible, you speak to a Christian friend, colleague or loved one for more information about Christianity.

Thanks again for bearing with me,
God bless you,
Jean

To sign up to Jean's blog and updates
on new books visit:
http://www.jeankabasomi.com.

For further information on
Jean's Christian clothing company,
Faith+Hope+Love visit:
http://www.faithhopelove13-13.com.

www.ingramcontent.com/pod-product-compliance
Lightning Source LLC
Chambersburg PA
CBHW052058070526
44584CB00017B/2245